GET
STARTED
IN FOOD
WRITING

Teach® Yourself

Get Started in Food Writing

Kerstin Rodgers

First published in Great Britain in 2015 by John Murray Learning. An Hachette UK company.

First published in US in 2015 by The McGraw-Hill Companies, Inc.

British Library Cataloguing in Publication Data: a catalogue record for this title is available from the British Library.

Library of Congress Catalog Card Number: on file.

Paperback ISBN 978 1 473 60036 2

Ebook ISBN 978 1 473 60038 6

1

The publisher has used its best endeavours to ensure that any website addresses referred to in this book are correct and active at the time of going to press. However, the publisher and the author have no responsibility for the websites and can make no guarantee that a site will remain live or that the content will remain relevant, decent or appropriate.

The publisher has made every effort to mark as such all words which it believes to be trademarks. The publisher should also like to make it clear that the presence of a word in the book, whether marked or unmarked, in no way affects its legal status as a trademark.

Every reasonable effort has been made by the publisher to trace the copyright holders of material in this book. Any errors or omissions should be notified in writing to the publisher, who will endeavour to rectify the situation for any reprints and future editions.

Typeset by Cenveo® Publisher Services.

Printed and bound in Great Britain by CPI Group (UK) Ltd., Croydon, CR0 4YY.

John Murray Learning policy is to use papers that are natural, renewable and recyclable products and made from wood grown in sustainable forests. The logging and manufacturing processes are expected to conform to the environmental regulations of the country of origin.

John Murray Learning
Carmelite House
50 Victoria Embankment
London EC4Y 0DZ
www.hodder.co.uk

Also available in ebook

Contents

About the author   vi

How to use this book   vii

1   Why write about food?   1

2   The 12 characteristics of the food writer   7

3   Types of food writing   17

4   A short history of food writing   43

5   How to write about food   51

6   Blogging about food   65

7   Promoting your food writing using social media   95

8   How to take great photographs of food   113

9   Earning money   131

10   Getting a book deal   143

11   Getting on TV and radio and how to make a cookery video   165

12   The future of food writing   189

Index   197

Acknowledgements   200

About the author

Kerstin Rodgers is a chef, author, blogger and photographer. In 2008 she started her award-winning blog msmarmitelover.com under her pseudonym msmarmitelover. In 2009 she started her supper club 'The Underground Restaurant', which launched an underground restaurant/supper club/pop-up movement around the UK and Europe. Kerstin runs a site called 'Find a Supper Club' (supperclubfangroup.ning.com) where people can find their local supper club.

As a photographer, she worked for the NME, record companies, Cosmopolitan, Elle, The Guardian and The Observer. She has also had exhibitions of her photography in Paris and London.

Kerstin has won awards: the Guild of Food Writers blog of the year in 2013 and the Fortnum & Mason online food writer of the year 2014. In 2011 she was named as one of London's 1,000 most influential people by the Evening Standard.

She has written three successful cookbooks: Supper Club: Recipes and Notes from the Underground Restaurant (HarperCollins 2011), MsMarmitelover's Secret Tea Party (Square Peg, 2014) and V is for Vegan (Quadrille, 2015).

How to use this book

The text is accompanied by a variety of boxes and exercises to help you develop and hone your food writing. These are indicated by the following icons:

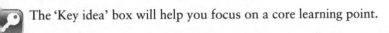 The 'Key idea' box will help you focus on a core learning point.

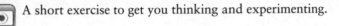 Words of advice and inspiration from cookery writers, bloggers and others.

A short exercise to get you thinking and experimenting.

An exercise that sets you a specific writing assignment.

An exercise that asks you to revisit, reassess and/or redo a piece of work.

A Workshop – a longer exercise or project.

1

Why write about food?

What is it about food that so many people including you, the purchaser of this book, want to write about it? Let's look around at what is happening in food.

It's the fashion!

Food is the new rock'n' roll. Currently we are all obsessed with food: TV seems to show nothing else but food programmes and celebrity chefs. It's so popular, you'd think cooking had just been invented.

The reasons for this are multiple: while television reflects the zeitgeist, it must be admitted that food programming is cheap to make, similar to reality TV. Many of the food shows are 'jeopardy'-based, which is TV lingo for turning cooking into a competition, a game show. Teaching people about food is no longer enough. We are encouraged to aspire to our own 15 minutes of food fame.

It's a whole other debate as to whether anybody is actually cooking more as a result of all this food programming but yes, gastronomy is all around us. In fact, there is even a new word for it, we are no longer eaters or cooks but 'foodies'.

People who have never worked or trained as cooks or worked in restaurants – soap actresses (Nadia Sawalha), TV presenters (Davina McCall), film stars (Gwyneth Paltrow, Alicia Silverstone), musicians (Cookin' with Coolio), musicians' kids (Mary McCartney, Daisy Lowe), models (Sophie Dahl, Lorraine Pascale, Daisy Lowe, Jasmine and Melissa Hemsley, Ella Woodward), wives (Tana Ramsay) and fashion experts (Gok Wan) – are now making food programmes, writing recipe books and newspaper columns on food.

And if they are not cooking and writing about it, they are talking about how *not* to eat food: the diet industry is huge. (This is a large and profitable sector so don't neglect that as a possible angle for your food writing. We will go into that further in Chapter 3.)

So it's no exaggeration to note that the last decade has been food-obsessed and it remains important to document that trend. Chefs are the new rock stars, restaurants are the places to go. My teenage daughter would rather go to a restaurant than go clubbing. As a food entrepreneur, I started night markets: farmers' markets held in the evening for young people to enjoy prepared dishes, shop for gourmet and artisan food, and listen to live music. My first one, which I called 'Tongue in Cheek' – a food rave – was held in my two-bedroomed apartment and in the garden. Starting after work on a Friday night: to my surprise, hundreds of young people queued for hours to get in. A very different audience to the married couples, parents and grandparents that go to farmers' markets on Sunday mornings.

When I was a teenager, I dreamed of writing and photographing for the *New Musical Express*. I spent my income on going to gigs, buying albums and hanging out in trendy bars. I hid the fact that I was interested in food: it wasn't hip. My handwritten recipe notebooks, complete with watercolours and drawings, were something only shamefully to be admitted to. Today young women are more likely to want to start a cupcake business.

Even children are starting food blogs: for example, nine-year-old Martha Payne whose blog, neverseconds.blogspot.com, documented her Scottish school dinners as well as what kids in other countries are eating for lunch. She was so successful she won awards and got a book deal on the back of her blog. Other youngsters are entering cooking competitions such as *Junior MasterChef* or hoping to go to cookery school. A couple of generations ago, catering college was where academic failures ended up. One chef in Leeds told me he was always in trouble as a teenager; finally the judge gave him a choice: a young offenders institution or cooking school. He chose the latter and, after training under Marco Pierre White, now has his own restaurant.

So how did this happen in a culture where one of the worst things you can be is overweight? As a vice, gluttony crowns the top seven deadly sins chart while the other six (pride, lust and greed particularly) are positively encouraged by capitalist society.

Is our food obsession the shadow side of the desire to be thin? We are conflicted: while overeating is frowned upon in Western culture, food is for the most part plentiful and ubiquitous. Food is cheaper than it used to be. The high street is no longer full of butchers, fishmongers and bakeries but cooked food outlets. Nowadays we want the finished object, fast food, the easy meal. More people live alone, meaning that it's an expensive effort to cook for yourself and almost cheaper to live on takeaways.

Food is now voyeurism, and food writing forms part of that. We eat with our eyes, almost a displacement activity. We want to read about it, see pictures, share Instagrams, tweet about our meals. In fact, a common criticism of Twitter one hears is: 'It is people tweeting about what they had for breakfast' – like that's a bad thing. It's entertainment. It's no coincidence that two of the most successful TV programmes of recent years are the globally imitated *Come Dine with Me* and *Bake Off,* the latter having the homely appeal of a Ms Marple-type thriller but with cake.

It's always been the fashion

Actually, food is all-important and always has been. One of the things I have noticed when travelling is how many folk songs and stories are about food and drink. Travelling through South America, where bus drivers have only one cassette played on a loop, lyrics about chicken and coconut embedded themselves in my mind through sheer repetition. At the time I thought: we sing about love, they croon about food.

Maybe we just fetishize it more nowadays, turn it into trends. The dirty burger or spiralized courgetti are just as much fashion victims as wedge heels or padded shoulders.

Something terrible happened to food in the last century and it's started to make us ill. The brave new world of factory-processed foods, big agriculture, supermarkets and labour-saving devices has revolutionized our lifestyles. But don't forget that we spent thousands of years making food, slowly, in the same way every day. Food is central to our religions, to our families, to our health. We are the only species on earth that cooks food – it's human behaviour at its most fundamental.

We are all experts

Food writing is a growth industry because we all eat approximately three times a day. Everyone, without exception, must eat, every day, for their entire lives. Even if you can only remember your mother's cooking, we all know about and have strong opinions on food.

It's not so much sex, death and taxes as food, sex and death that are the driving force behind humanity. And let's face it: food is more readily available than sex. It's a primary necessity.

Even if you don't cook, you have to eat. Dining out involves a quick mental count of the last time you ate such and such, going to the food establishment in question, ordering the food, eating it and returning home.

Food is time consuming. It can take you an hour and a half to cook it but just ten minutes to eat it. While food can be seen as an art form, and some chefs are lauded as great artists, it is ephemeral. Food writing attempts to pin it down.

If sleeping takes up a third of our lives, food must occupy at least a quarter. I'm not just talking about eating it: think of the time spent shopping it, unloading it, planning it, preparing it, cooking it, and cleaning it all up afterwards. And the whole process is repeated three hours later.

Food is culture, food is history

The arc of human development is characterized by the discovery of fire, the engineering of pots and utensils and the art and science of cooking. Cooking enabled us to extract more nutrients from food, made it more digestible, leading, on an evolutionary level, to the large human brain. Hunting, gathering, agriculture, through to the modern day – we are distinguished by what we eat and how. The earliest economics, the spice trade for instance, is related to food and the desire for new tastes. The word 'salary' derives from a basic foodstuff: salt. Roman soldiers were paid in salt, a precious commodity. Writing about the history of food, travelling and discovering new dishes are all great material for food writers.

The differences even between America and Europe are worth discussion: fast food versus slow food? Some statistics suggest that Americans spend 75 minutes a day eating, whereas Europeans feast for over two hours.

Perhaps the less we cook, the more we want to read about cooking, eating, drinking, consuming. Certainly, there is no shortage of food-related subjects to write about. This is where you come in. In this book we will be talking about the meat and veg of food writing.

Snapshot exercise

Experiment with mindful eating. Notice what you eat. Write notes on it; take pictures. When you next cook something, write it up as a recipe, as if you were teaching someone who didn't know how to cook.

Key idea

Read. Read food magazines, big and small, from *Delicious* and *Olive* to *Lucky Peach*, a quarterly started by Momofuku's David Chang, or *Cherry Bombe*, a biannual that celebrates women in food. Read newspaper articles on food. Read blogs, both general and specialist. I recommend TheKitchn.com as a large generalized food blog written by paid journalists and at the other end of the scale, http://azeliaskitchen.net, who is a non-professional who writes with a detailed, scientific zeal about baking bread.

And finally, don't just read cookbooks but also books about food that don't include recipes. Don't just read the recipes, read the introductory chapters. Read cookery writers who've appeared throughout history: Elizabeth David as well as Jamie Oliver.

Food is an important subject to write about. The angles you can explore within food are almost never-ending. You don't have to have a lot of money, incredible cooking skills or a large budget for exotic ingredients. You can write about the slice of toast you had for breakfast this morning. You can write about your local discount supermarket. In fact, the more specialized angle you adopt, rather than just the cliché of going to posh restaurants, the more likely you will come to the attention of commissioning editors and publishers.

Next step

In the next chapter we look at the 12 characteristics of the typical food writer.

2

The 12 characteristics of the food writer

In this chapter you will look at the characteristics of the food writer and, no doubt, their readers.

1 Hungry

It really helps if you like eating. That might sound curious, but some people, believe it or not, are just not that interested in food, for them it's merely fuel. Some people, on the other hand, may be interested in food but have a limited diet, like coeliacs. Other food writers may have a disability, like chef and author Marlena Spieler, who had an accident in which she lost her sense of taste and has since been documenting her journey back to taste. A unique perspective can be essential to interesting food writing.

2 Curious

You must be driven to learn more about your chosen subject. New and old food experiences, from family meals to the latest restaurant trend, can form part of your writing.

Take a small subject, say sugar, and research it. Where does it come from? What different types of sugar are there? Do they taste different? Why are we addicted to it? The possibilities are endless. Do not, however, simply rely on Wikipedia. There was a talented but young journalist who was writing a regular food column in a top newspaper. It was clear that he was using Wikipedia to get many of his facts. His nickname in the food world became 'Consider Wikipedia'. Wikipedia is useful, but use it as a starting point only. Go visit, do interviews, ask questions, don't just do all your research on the Internet, convenient as that may be. Everyone else will have access to the same information, the only way to make your work distinctive is to do field research of your own.

3 Fat

Yes. Food writing makes you fat. I remember meeting a bunch of other food bloggers around 2009 at various events in London. They were all fairly normally shaped. Two years later, on another trip, most of them could barely waddle around the restaurants to which we'd received freebie invitations. Some of them got disciplined and went on whatever fad diet was going around at the time: the 5:2 diet, the Dukan Diet, juicing or raw diets. Some of us, like me, who already had a propensity to being overweight, got extra fat and stayed there. Food writing can be injurious to your health! Just sayin'!

4 Practical

While it depends on what kind of food writing you intend to concentrate on, hands-on practicality is always preferable to the purely theoretical. I never write about things that I haven't personally done or experienced. Cooking itself is practical and testing recipes, or creating them, is always important in the field of food writing. Cooking is an alchemy, a mixture of science and art. Cooking is how most people learn about science, which is why in school it is called 'Domestic Science'. There is little difference between experimenting with dry versus wet caramel on your stove, or fermenting sauerkraut or sourdough, or butchering an animal and physics, chemistry or biology as taught in the education system. When science was not open to women, domestic science was how we learned.

If you are basically a writer rather than a cook, you will need to up your practical skills in the kitchen. It's hard to write about food if you've never made any! Take a course or force yourself to cook. Perhaps choose a cookbook and work your way through it. Take a case study like Dan Toombs, also known as The Curry Guy, of the eponymous blog. Originally from California, he married a British wife and moved to Yorkshire 20 years ago. Dan's background is in computer merchandise so he had the technical know-how to start a food blog as a hobby in 2010. He knew little about Indian food but enjoyed its spiciness which reminded him of the Mexican food he ate and cooked back in the States. (There isn't much Mexican immigration to Yorkshire but thanks to the IT industry, there is increasing Indian emigration to Silicon Valley in California and, as a result, more Indian restaurants.) Dan remarks that many ingredients in Mexican and Indian food are similar, spread by Portuguese explorers. Trouble was, eating takeaways and in curry houses was starting to become very expensive for his large family. As the family's main cook, in 2011 he set out to cook only Indian food for a year and blog about it. Gradually, famous Indian chefs such as Vivek Singh and Atul Kochhar got to hear about his curry 'journey' and invited him to learn to cook dishes in their restaurant kitchens. Eventually, Dan got to know the difference between BIR (British Indian Restaurant) food and the vast range of authentic Subcontinental cooking.

BIR, Dan learned, emanated from the post-colonial immigration from India and Pakistan and later, in the 1970s, refugees from the Bangladeshi Liberation War and the Ugandan Asian phase of migration to the UK. Often it was the men of the families who came first, bringing their wives and children later. These men were not trained chefs and, in their culture, didn't even do the cooking; it was the women who did it. They opened restaurants not knowing how to cook and in the 1960s and 1970s there weren't many authentic Asian ingredients for sale in Britain. The different spices were not available, rather there was a generic curry powder. They created a bland stock curry sauce that was onion based with a little bit of tomato and not much heat. All the restaurants used the same recipes. Today's Indian restaurant cooking is far more authentic, fresher and more varied.

Dan was invited to speak at the World Curry Festival in Bradford. He's written an ebook and is currently in talks to get an offline book published. His hobby has started to become a small business, a second income; most of his blog posts are sponsored. His tips on how to improve your blog ratings are given later in the book.

Not knowing how to cook is also worth writing about. Esther Walker's blog Recipe Rifle is about learning how to cook. As the newly married wife of Giles Coren, the famous restaurant critic, no less, she felt under pressure to acquire some cooking skills very quickly. Her self-deprecating, clever and amusing writing has thousands of readers.

5 Professional

Have a professional attitude. Even if you are working for no money, for instance if you are blogging, act as if you are getting paid. Write every day and blog regularly. If writing for others, stick to the word count. Check your spelling and grammar. Get your facts right and do the research. Meet your deadlines. Try to keep procrastination to a minimum.

6 Intellectual

I don't think a food writer *has* to be intellectual. You need enough intellect to be able to think things through and write them down but a more crucial quality is sensuality. Eating isn't just about survival; it's sensual, too. In my own writing, experience is the essential component. I don't have an intellectual or academic viewpoint, I'm more like a reporter. I try to accurately and minutely describe the details of a restaurant or a food experience or the process of cooking a recipe. Nonetheless, for some writing, you may take an intellectual stance; for the ethical food essay or for more scientific writing.

7 Nostalgic

I have noticed that many food writers are nostalgic; when they think of the past, their childhood or a trip, it's the food they focus on. Food and family are inextricably linked – our mother's cooking, growing up, comfort food, Sunday lunch. Food is a souvenir, both in the French sense of a memory and in the British sense of holding on to something concrete from a faraway place.

8 Political

Food writing can be political. The austerity blogger Jack Monroe is a case in point. As an impoverished single mother on benefits, she blogged about having to go to food banks to feed herself and her three-year-old son. With a weekly food budget of £10, she wrote about meals for under a pound, itemizing the cost of each ingredient. Her blog was picked up by *The Guardian*, she got a food column, she wrote a best-selling austerity cookbook and she was invited on *Question Time* and to Parliament. Another example, the award-winning food writer Alex Renton is political about the ethics of food, writing about vegetarianism, the abuses of big supermarkets and how they treat farmers. You may be passionate about local farmers, about organic food, about animal rights. Or you might feel just as strongly about hunting, the preservation of the countryside, or that GM (genetically modified) foods are in fact the right way to go for a rapidly expanding global population. Your politics can be included in your food writing or even be used as a structuring framework.

9 Personal

I always like the personal. But not the relentless whinging, moaning and self-obsession that some writers can indulge in – no, you must always reference the exterior world too, the facts. Intimate details always bring a subject home to the reader; you achieve relatability. In the pure journalistic style, you never use 'I' but this can make for rather dry reading. You want to connect with the reader; therefore you must be willing to open up. I once wrote a blog post about feeling depressed and what foods help depression. It immediately got hits and comments. I felt so exposed when I wrote it but you have to be brave. The likes of columnist Liz Jones, who is not a food writer (but has strong feelings about food, having been anorexic and now vegan), says that if it doesn't hurt when you publish, it's not worth publishing. She is known for her extreme honesty, which can make her columns difficult to read but she is never less than riveting. She also suffers personal abuse. When you open up to the world, this is a risk, especially if you are a woman writer. But she is one of Fleet Street's highest-paid columnists so she's doing something right.

Ascertain the level of exposure you can handle. But consider that your privacy boundaries are likely to expand as you continue writing. Even if you are criticized, there will also be positive feedback in which people express their gratitude for your honesty. This is very rewarding, particularly as the encouraging readers often outnumber the critics.

10 Romantic

I think we all romanticize the idea of being a writer. Sometimes we want what we perceive to be the lifestyle of a writer rather than do the hard graft of sitting down alone in a silent room, not going out and writing every day.

Ernest Hemingway has been very bad for writing, although I admire his pared-down prose. Let me explain why. I had a friend when I was living in France – let's call him Si. He was an English ex-pat who wanted to write and to that end he moved to a small village in the south of France because, of course, you can't do it in the suburbs of Manchester. His writing hero was Hemingway. Meeting him in a local café (I was staying in France at the time), I started to tell Si about my first book deal; I was very excited to share the news. He waved me away: 'I'm not interested in women's writing.'

He then brought out a few crumpled pages from his back pocket with a story pencilled in tiny writing all over them. Everyone at our table lost interest in my actual real-life book deal and expressed interest in Si's 'important' writing. Si read it out. The story was based on one of many incidents where Si gets drunk, sleeps with various women around the village, upsets most of the women in the village and wakes up in a ditch with no money having lost his coat. Everyone was terribly impressed. This is a real writer, they thought. This was the only thing Si had written in six months. It was pretty clichéd, to be frank. Si had a terrible drink problem and treated women shabbily in real life. But for him and his mates, he was living the writer's dream. But the truth is he's never been published and his productivity is extremely low. I still have hopes for him – he's a nice guy at heart – but he'd committed the fatal error of falling in love with the lifestyle of a writer rather than doing the work. Writing is not glamorous; it's kind of boring and lonely. It's psychologically painful, even. You can't always wait for the muse. To be a writer, just bash it out.

11 Trained

You don't have to be trained but it can help.

JOURNALISTIC TRAINING

For journalism training, check the National Council for the Training of Journalists (NCTJ) site (www.nctj.com). There are courses run all over the UK. A year-long course costs between £2,500 and £4,500, depending on your age.

For specific courses in food writing, here are a couple of suggestions: try the CityLit in London (www.citylit.ac.uk), which does a day course costing around £55, or the week-long residential courses run by Arvon (www.arvon.org), about which I have heard good things. You can apply to these courses for grants if you have a low income.

COOKING COURSES

Depending on the kind of food writing you want to do, you may want to improve your cooking skills. The best and most elite cookery courses can be very expensive, around £20,000 a year. There are some bursaries, but some of the people attending will be rich, bored housewives and academically deficient posh kids, perhaps getting a vocational course to become a chalet girl. If you are really broke, go to catering college or, better still, get a job in a restaurant and work your way up through all the cooking stations. You will learn more in a month at even the humblest restaurant than you will in a year at most colleges in terms of the reality of a life in food. But it's probably best to combine theory and practical techniques learned on a course with some real-life experience. Young ambitious chefs do 'stages' (work experience) in three-month tranches around the world, going from the Fat Duck to Noma to Japan and the top restaurants in the States. This requires dedication and persistence.

High-end cooking courses include:

- **Le Manoir aux Quat'Saisons (www.belmond.com/le-manoir-aux-quat-saisons-oxfordshire)**. A friend of my mum went there. It cost a packet but she highly recommended it. A member of Pink Floyd was on the course with her. You will learn classical French cookery.
- **Leiths (www.leiths.com)**. This famous cookery school in London has an illustrious alumni: Gizzi Erskine, Diana Henry, Xanthe Clay, Florence Knight, Sam Clark (the male half; his wife is called Sam Clark too) of the restaurant Moro. It runs both professional and amateur (or enthusiasts') courses, from a year-long diploma to day courses. They also do food-styling courses.
- **Ballymaloe (www.cookingisfun.ie)**. This Cork-based cookery school in Ireland is run by the Allen family, headed by Darina Allen. They do year-long courses and one-term courses.
- **Cordon Vert (www.cordonvert.co.uk)**. This vegetarian cookery school in London and Cheshire runs a year-long professional diploma as well as shorter courses.
- **Billingsgate Seafood Training School (www.seafoodtraining. org)**. Courses here are run by a retired fishmonger. I did one with a fishmonger and fish smoker named Ken Condon who had great insight on how to choose your fish and also great gossipy anecdotes. They have several half-day to two-day courses. I did

a short course. It was absolutely fascinating and I learned so much in just one day.

- **WSET (Wine & Spirits Education Trust; www.wsetglobal.com).** This offers Level 1 to Level 5 diploma. Its courses are held everywhere in the UK.

12 A traveller

You can learn and write about food just in your immediate area, which is interesting in itself, but most foodies are interested in international cuisine. I get many of my ideas for dishes when I travel. My trips provide the backdrop to, and the in-depth knowledge for, my articles.

However, living in London (or any big city) is a constant journey around the world. Almost every type of food is sold, whether in shops, delicatessens or restaurants. Just in my area of Kilburn I have Polish, Romanian, Kurdish, Armenian, Bulgarian, Indian, Sri Lankan, Pakistani and Chinese shops. I can pretend to be in Afghanistan, Iran, southern India, Poland, France, Italy, the Caribbean, virtually any night of the week by dint of visiting a different restaurant within a mile or so of my house.

A blogger and author Helen Graves, who writes Food Stories, lives in Peckham, South London. It's a poor but cosmopolitan part of London which is rapidly becoming trendy. She often blogs about the Caribbean and African restaurants and markets near where she lives. She even makes and sells her own jerk sauce via her blog.

I love to travel and I love to learn languages. I can speak fluent French, pretty good Spanish and can manage in Portuguese and Italian. Every country I visit, I try to learn a few phrases. In terms of the food world, it helps to be open to learning a foreign language.

However, be careful about sounding pretentious in your writing by using too many foreign, particularly French, terms of cuisine. It can sound comedic.

Next step

In the following chapter we will be looking at the different types of food writing.

3

Types of food writing

In this chapter we will look at the different types of food writing. There are more avenues to go down than you might think, from restaurant reviews and recipe writing to speciality/industry/trade press food writing. Chances are, your image of a food writer is somebody writing a restaurant review. Of course, this is an essential part of the food writing spectrum but there is a great deal more to it.

Restaurant reviews

The main job of restaurant critics is to entertain us. If, in addition, they actually know something about food, then that is an added bonus. And, of course, the good critics – those who develop a great reputation – are the ones who can do both: they write wittily and with insight, knowing how a dish should be cooked, whether it was cooked correctly and whether the restaurant has conveyed the dish with accuracy. The critic has most likely travelled to the country of origin, so they'll know whether that spaghetti vongole was done just right. Their years of experience will lend their reviews depth and authenticity. But, at the same time, they are funny and absorbing to read; no one wants to read a dry piece full of technical knowledge but with no flair.

The newspaper audience is not the same as that for a trade magazine or even a blog, for the latter tend to attract people particularly interested in their subject. The newspaper restaurant critic is selling newspapers rather than restaurants. Nevertheless, without a doubt, a restaurant review in a major newspaper makes a huge difference to the restaurant. A good review from, say, Jay Rayner in *The Observer*, will mean that the restaurant will be booked up for weeks, if not months. It marks the difference between a going concern and a flop.

Impressing restaurant critics is so important that restaurants will keep laminated photos of the known critics on the walls of the kitchen so that staff recognize them when they walk in. Nowadays the smart restaurant will even google the names of diners so it knows who is who. A New York restaurant admits to doing precisely that: Eleven Madison Park googles every single guest before they arrive.

 ## Manager of Eleven Madison Park

'If I find out a guest is from Montana, and I know we have a server from there, we'll put them together.'

An article about restaurants doesn't just have to be about the food; it can be about the service, the owner, the ethos. This is the future. Faced with food bloggers, Instagrammers, citizen journalism as well as restaurant reviews by ordinary people on sites such as Trip Advisor, a restaurant can no longer get away with doing a poor job. They will quickly get found out.

I have to admit that, if I'm at a restaurant and getting poor service, I find that taking a few pictures of the food does wonders. They immediately start to wonder who you are, whether you are 'somebody'.

THE BEHEMOTHS OF RESTAURANT REVIEWING

The following critics bestride the restaurant industry like behemoths and it is well worth reading their reviews on a regular basis:

- Jay Rayner of *The Observer* – a long-time journalist who has for some years specialized in the food industry. He writes well, clearly likes his dinner, and is also concerned about ethical issues within the food industry.
- Giles Coren of *The Times* – the *enfant terrible* of restaurant reviewing.
- Fay Maschler of the *Evening Standard* – the *grande dame* of restaurant reviewing who has been working for the *Standard* for over 40 years.
- A.A. Gill of *The Sunday Times* – to my mind, the funniest and most savage of the restaurant reviewers.
- Marina O'Loughlin of *The Guardian* – kind but funny with fantastic food knowledge, particularly of her beloved Italy.

MARINA'S TOP TIPS FOR BECOMING A RESTAURANT REVIEWER

- 'Have a rich mummy and daddy or marry well. This is an expensive profession. Even when you get paid, you don't get paid much.'
- There are no openings as a restaurant critic in the main publications. 'You'll have to wait until one of us dies.' Working for local papers, magazines or starting your own blog are virtually the only ways of getting into the field.
- People are only interested in London. Although there are frequent complaints that *The Guardian* reviews are too

London-centric, the stats (or viewing figures) go down dramatically when Marina reviews a restaurant elsewhere in the country. The reasons for this include: London has a large population with more disposable income, therefore a larger restaurant-going public. London has many tourists and visitors from around the world who are also interested in which restaurants to visit in the city. Thirdly, London is a trendsetter: what London does is what the rest of the country will do in a few years' time. All of the UK looks to London, like it or not, for what's happening in food. On the positive side, this means that there is an opportunity for people who don't live in London to carve out their own niche. If London critics aren't getting to provincial restaurants, there are still readers who want to know about those restaurants.

- People think reviewers are puppets of the PR industry. This isn't true. Good reviewers, respected reviewers, are independent.

- 'Eat at every restaurant you can for 20 years.' Marina has been at this game for a long time – that's one of the reasons she got the job. She loves restaurants more than food. She likes the service, the style of the tableware, the architecture, everything about restaurants. There is a distinction between food writing and restaurant writing; it's not just food. Some restaurants don't have great food but you love them. Some restaurants do have great food, but no atmosphere. 'So many restaurants aren't fun anymore,' complains Marina. She laments restaurants that aren't interested in the diner but are all about the celebrity or artistry of the chef.

- Go into PR. If you love eating at restaurants and don't have the money to do so, working in restaurant PR is a way of getting into the field.

- Don't write about yourself. Unless you are a celebrity, nobody is interested in you. Make anything personal contextual.

- Eat abroad. Think internationally. You need to know what Thai food is like in Thailand.

- Get experience in the food industry. Marina worked in restaurants for ten years. This gave her an insider's knowledge and meant that she was able to judge more effectively the strengths and weaknesses of the restaurant.

- Get experience as a journalist or writer. Marina worked as a copywriter in advertising prior to becoming a restaurant reviewer. So she got used to working to a brief, working quickly and sticking to her word count.

- Marina doesn't take notes in the restaurant: she takes photographs with her phone. This acts as an aide-mémoire and doesn't draw attention to her as a reviewer.

- Before visiting a restaurant and writing a review, Marina doesn't read any other reviews. She will do research, say, into Argentinian food before visiting an Argentinian restaurant. She reads other people's reviews only after she has written her piece.

- You must have the courage of your convictions, have your own voice.

Snapshot exercise

Try writing reviews for sites like Trip Advisor – it is excellent practice. Trip Advisor reviewers can wield remarkable power. The *Daily Mail* ran a story on Britain's most feared restaurant critic, a travelling salesman from Newcastle who eats out every day as he is rarely at home. He has written a whopping 780 restaurant reviews for Trip Advisor. He'll review anything from a local branch of McDonalds to Michelin-starred restaurants in Venice. This makes him one of the UK's most prolific restaurant reviewers. You could say he is even more influential than the broadsheet restaurant reviewers by the sheer scale of his reviewing.

AVOIDING CLICHÉS IN RESTAURANT REVIEWS

There is a certain type of vocabulary used only in restaurant reviews, which as a beginner you may be prone to adopt. Try to avoid the following terms and expressions:

- 'my companion', to refer to your friend, partner or family member sitting at the table with you
- commensurate – fancy-pants word for 'worth the money'
- delicious – use rarely
- tasty – use only sometimes
- yummy – use even more rarely
- 'Nom nom nom' – never use this
- washed down with
- cuts through…
- accompanied by…
- tucks into…
- lip-smacking
- sinful/decadent dessert
- perfect foil
- Proustian – as in Marcel Proust's extensive memory trip inspired by a bite of a madeleine. Food does evoke memories, but try to use other expressions.
- lashings of
- 'The … did not disappoint.'
- plumped for – use 'chose'
- opted for – ditto
- 'Chef suggested that we try…'
- 'The X was to die for…'
- 'enrobed' – a bit Hobbity
- cooked to perfection
- saved room for
- delectable
- meltingly tender
- an array of…

Key idea

In *The Washington Post*, writer Emily Badger describes the difference of language used for expensive restaurants as opposed to cheap ones. Sensual and sexual vocabulary (sinful, pornographic, orgasmic) is employed for high-end, upscale restaurants while drugs imagery (addiction, crack, bingeing, craving) is the most frequently used analogy for cheap food.

Write exercise

Writing about restaurants requires a budget, especially when starting out. You could write about fast food or cheap restaurants in your area.

Go to a McDonalds, Burger King or other fast-food establishment and describe the meal, in a 250-word review, as if it were a Michelin-star experience. Feel free to use the banned phrases listed above. Make it as pretentious as possible, using French expressions such as 'coulis' for the tomato ketchup.

Edit exercise

Now do the same thing but write it as it was, using ordinary unpretentious non-restaurant language.

Write exercise

Describe a home-cooked meal or a dinner party that you have attended as if you were going to a restaurant in 500 words. Do not use any of the banned phrases. It can be critical or affectionate. You can make observations on the host and other guests as well as the food. Describe the 'service'.

BAD REVIEWS

There was a case back in 2007 where Irish food critic Caroline Workman poorly reviewed Belfast restaurant Goodfellas for *The Irish News*. The restaurant sued for libel and, at first, won. There were worries that the 'profession' of restaurant reviewing would have to cease. Fortunately, the decision was reversed on appeal. In an article in *The Guardian* commenting on the case, Jay Rayner explained: 'If I say that the soup must have been made from a packet, and it wasn't, that's a libel. If I say – as, more or less, I once did – that a soup tasted as if it had been made from a packet, which is remarkable given that they must have made it themselves, that is not a libel.'

While you are at liberty to express exactly what you think about the restaurant, be factually accurate.

Cookery and recipe writing

 Stephen King, *On Writing*

'Colonel Saunders made an awful lot of fried chicken, but I'm not sure anyone wanted to know how to make it.'

This part of the book is for the writers who do want to know how to make the fried chicken.

Cookery and recipe writing is the other most popular type of food writing. One of the single biggest terms that attract traffic on the Internet is the word 'recipe'. How to cook stuff, explained step by step, will always be popular.

Recipe writing is a mix of art and science. The art is in the introductory passage, the idea and inspiration behind the recipe while the science lies in making sure that the recipe instructions are easy to understand and that the recipe works. Cookery classes in school used to be called Domestic Science for a reason. When I am testing a complicated recipe and using unusual ingredients such as soy lecithin to make my own vegan margarine, this is science enacted within the domestic sphere. One could say that this is how the majority of women (who do most cooking and are underrepresented in science – both at university and professionally) learn science, through cookery.

HOW TO WRITE AN INTRODUCTION TO A RECIPE

The typical introduction to a recipe is a memory. Sometimes it's a childhood memory, 'I remember my mother baking this cake for my sister's birthday', or a holiday or travel memory: 'It was in Crete that I first ate dolmades.' (Many of us only eat out regularly when on holiday.) Another introduction refers to the seasonality of the ingredients, as in 'This ingredient is seasonal right now and therefore I decided to make an asparagus frittata.' Perhaps it's something you've grown in your garden/allotment that is now ready to eat.

Best-selling UK cookery writers Nigella Lawson and Nigel Slater have a clear 'voice'. You actually imagine them speaking to you through the written word. David Sexton of the *Evening Standard* describes their style thus:

> Nigel and Nigella's [...] books are quite simply and exclusively about what they themselves like to eat and thus cook. Neither of them ever professes to be concerned about cooking in any particular tradition or in the style of any particular region. They're not just a bit eclectic, they're weirdly, wonderfully, self-centred. When you cook from their books, you really are cooking not Italian or Thai, but a Nigel or Nigella, nothing less.

These are writers who use the first person, with an almost confessional style, when approaching food. Many bloggers, myself included, take inspiration from this.

Nigel Slater

'I have always felt that a recipe is more than a set of instructions. Some readers use recipes purely as a means to an end. They want explicitly detailed "1, 2, 3" directions. But others read them like a novel and want more than a formula that leads to a result.'

Snapshot exercise

Think about how readable your writing is. Is it easy to understand? Is your recipe easy to follow?

A study by the Department for Innovation, Universities and Skills (DIUS) suggested that Nigel Slater is the easiest recipe writer to understand. Nigella Lawson's strings of adjectives make her harder to understand, necessitating a higher educational level. Male cookery writers, it is claimed, are more direct. I find that a strange claim considering the vast hidden army of middle-aged female ghostwriters belonging to the Guild of Food Writers who actually write the nation's food books and food columns. Generally, the food industry is also divided down gender lines: chefs are men; cookery writers are women.

WRITING THE RECIPE

After the introduction, some recipes detail the time required to make the recipe; this can be divided into prep time and cooking time. Some recipes also describe the skill level necessary to cook the recipe (e.g. 'Easy' or 'for the experienced cook'). I tend to mention in the introduction how easy or difficult the recipe will be to make and how much time to set aside. I like to prepare readers.

Another section you can add is about the equipment needed. Some authors write down the equipment for each recipe, I tend only to mention it when the recipe requires specialist equipment or, say, a particular size or type of cake tin. For instance, if you are making madeleines, you really do need a madeleine baking tin. If the recipe is for ice cream, I would assume that most people would have an ice-cream maker. Some cookbooks, however, will also give instructions on how to make the ice cream without an ice-cream maker.

One piece of equipment you cannot assume everyone has is a stand mixer. You will need to give instructions for using both a stand mixer and for making it by hand. You, as a keen cook, will likely possess one, but your reader may not. Do you want to alienate the beginner cook, or the poor cook, or the casual cook, by not telling them how to make the recipe unless they have a £400 stand mixer or food processor?

After that, recipes are divided into 'ingredients' and 'method'.

The order of ingredients is very important. You might assume, for instance, that, if you are making coq au vin, chicken, being the central ingredient of the dish, would be the first thing listed under 'ingredients'. Wrong. The ingredients must be listed in order of use. In James Martin's recipe for coq au vin on the BBC website, chicken is actually the tenth ingredient out of 12. Why is this? Because Martin first has to make the sauce, using the butter, the shallots, the bacon, the herbs, the mushrooms, the wine, the stock and so on.

Snapshot exercise

Imagine you are making burgers with home-made buns and quick pickled onions, and write down what the order of the ingredients would be.

As the buns take longer than anything else, you would list the bun ingredients first. So, you would make a list: flour, water, salt and seeds, depending on your recipe.

Next you would list the ingredients for the quick pickled onions. These take maybe half an hour to an hour to make and you would prep them before the burger. So you would write: red onions, vinegar, salt, sugar.

Finally, you write the ingredients for the burgers: onions, meat, egg, salt, pepper.

To save words and time when writing the method, describe the preparation of the ingredient in the ingredient list (e.g. 'onions, sliced thinly'). This eliminates the need to say in the method: 'First slice your onions thinly.'

WEIGHTS AND MEASURES

Measures are an important part of recipe writing, and it can be a sticky subject, especially when it concerns the difference between UK and US styles.

David Lebowitz

'I think everyone in America, when they're born, should be handed a scale.'

In general, the United States likes to cook by volume rather than by weight, unlike Europe which prefers the latter. Americans even talk of 'tablespoons' of butter. A 2008 article in the *Wall Street Journal* states that US cookbook publishers think that for Americans, 'weights tend to look daunting'. One British cookbook editor told me that an American reader complained that 'every time you insist that I weigh something, I have to go down to the Post Office to use their scales'. Americans, despite the cheap price of digital scales, simply don't have them in their kitchen. This can lead, in American recipes, to bizarre combinations of measurements like 'one cup and half a teaspoon of flour'. I worked with an American cook at one of my supper clubs, Terry Hope Romero, and while I was out shopping, I returned to find her using my laundry scoop as a 'cup', so desperate was she to find a tool similar to the one she used at home.

The distinction is not always so clear-cut. The English cookbook writer Nigella Lawson famously adores – even sells through her homeware line – the American system of cups and she helpfully provides a conversion scale in the back of her books. Conversely, the legendary aforementioned American cook Alice Waters in *The Art of Simple Food* (2007) stresses the importance of weighing and scales.

Although I can understand the appeal of being able to picture an amount you might need for a recipe, I agree with Alice Waters: a cup of flour is different depending on the weather, the humidity, the shakiness of your hand that day, the amount of gunk that is stuck in the bottom of your chosen container after the second or third cup. All these factors can affect the success of your recipe. I've worked out an American cup (even their cup sizes are different from ours) is 150g of flour, but Nigella says it's 140g, Australian cookbook author Donna Hay says it's 135g and the *Wall Street Journal* article says 120g sifted. That can make the difference between wasted time and ingredients; failure and success.

When you write recipes you have a responsibility. A bad recipe that doesn't work means your reader has wasted their money.

Key idea

Precision in measurements, especially in baking, is essential. French baker Richard Bertinet is so keen on accuracy that he even recommends weighing water in grams rather than measuring millilitres in a jug. Those casual references in recipes to a pinch of salt (1/16th of a teaspoon), a dash (1/8th) of vanilla essence, a smidgeon (1/32th) of spice, a glug (a very quick down-and-up pour) of oil are, in fact, micro measurements not to be taken lightly.

Another method of recipe writing and measuring is explained in *Ratio: The Simple Codes behind the Craft of Everyday Cooking* by American author Michael Ruhlman who takes the traditional 1-2-3-4 (butter, sugar, flour, eggs) American cup ratio recipe for making a cake and applies it to all cooking. Ruhlman says that the following ratio for bread will 'unchain you from recipes': 5 parts flour; 3 parts water (plus yeast and salt). Change this ratio slightly – 3 parts flour, 2 parts egg – and it becomes pasta dough.

Metric or imperial?

I like the imperial inches, feet and yards as they are based on the natural measurements of the human body: an inch is a thumb (in French the words 'inch' and 'thumb' are identical: *pouce*), a yard is the distance between the end of your nose and the fingers of your arm outstretched. However, in cooking I use grams and litres rather than the ounces and pounds of my childhood.

Snapshot exercise

What system do you use to measure? Are you comfortable with cups? Or do you groove to grams? How do you measure up? Take an American recipe using volume and convert it to grams. Then

take a weighed/gram recipe you know well and convert it to cups/
sticks/spoons. Take a cup of flour, loosely filled and then weigh it.
How much does it weigh?

Note that down. Now pack the cup tightly with flour, how much
does that weigh? See the difference?

Cook or bake this converted recipe. Does it work as well? Note
the differences.

THE METHOD

This is the set of instructions on what to do with the ingredients.
Starting from the top of your ingredient list, write short, clear
sentences describing exactly what your reader must do to cook/
prepare this dish. Cooking has a specific vocabulary – you need to
know the terms.

Term	Meaning
barbecue	to cook food outside on wood or charcoal
beat	to stir vigorously
blanch and shock	to boil a vegetable or fruit very quickly then plunge into cold water.
boil	to cook things in boiling water, thereby retaining colour
braise and stew	to braise is to cook food for a short time in a small amount of liquid; to stew is to cook for a longer time in a sauce or liquid
caramelize	to cook until brown and soft, developing a Maillard reaction
combine	to mix together ingredients
cream	to beat to make butter, sugar and eggs creamy
cut in	to add butter to flour, in pastry work
fold	to stir in a figure of eight, carefully, so as to keep in the air
grill	to cook food over a high heat so that the food cooks quicker on the outside
knead	to pull and push bread dough so that the gluten is activated
prove	to leave dough to rise
roast	to cook food in the oven with a small amount of oil
sauté and fry	to sauté is to fry food in a small amount of oil; to fry is to cook in a larger amount of oil, for longer
scrape down	using a spatula, scrape down the sides of a bowl
soft and stiff peaks	when whisking eggs and sugar the peaks are described as 'soft' when they are still able to flop over

soften/sweat	to cook onions etc. until soft
steam	to cook food over, but not in, boiling water
stir	to mix in a circular movement
stir-fry	the Asian version of sautéing; to cook quickly
temper	to fry small amounts of spices; to heat and cool chocolate to make it as smooth as possible; to add egg to custard
toss	to lightly mix in a sauce or liquid, usually with reference to a salad
whip	to incorporate air into cream
whisk	using a whisk, to mix together and add air

OTHER KEY ISSUES

What size saucepan, baking tin, cake tin?

Think about the quantities you are cooking plus the eventual amount. No point telling the reader to start cooking in a small saucepan if eventually, with all the ingredients, the amount will need a large saucepan. Readers want to avoid washing up. With baking, accuracy is even more important. The success of many cake recipes relies on the size of the cake tin.

Find out the standard sizes. Be aware that people are less likely to cook your recipe if you are using something they do not already possess in their kitchen cupboard. A supermarket that sells cookware will be a good guide to this. For instance, the classic sandwich tin is 8 inches (20cm) across. So try not to do a recipe for a 7-inch (18-cm) tin unless absolutely necessary. Or give quantities for both.

Delia Smith, 'The Tyranny of Tins'

'I could write a whole book just on this subject. Over the years I have constantly had to re-jig cake recipes because the required tin sizes were no longer available. And this is the predominant reason more often than not that cake recipes sometimes fail – that is, you are simply not using the correct tin for the mixture.'

Know your utensils

Do they need a rubber spatula, wooden spoon, fish slice?

What level of heat?

Do tell the reader what level of heat they will need for each stage of the recipe – e.g. 'Fry the tomatoes in a small saucepan on a medium heat.' Tell them also when to turn the heat down to a simmer.

Preheating the oven

The oven needs to be at the right temperature once the recipe is assembled so you will need to ask the reader to preheat the oven. At what point do you do this? Mostly you will see 'Preheat the oven to 200 °C', for instance, at the beginning of the recipe. But if the recipe requires a lengthy process before baking, you may want to ask the reader to 'preheat the oven' at a later point in the method. Most ovens require 15 to 30 minutes to get up to the correct temperature, depending on the type of oven. So, in your recipe, tell the reader to preheat the oven approximately 15 to 30 minutes before they need to use it.

For absolutely accurate temperatures, calibrate your oven. Buy a cheap oven thermometer and turn your oven up to its highest heat. (This will take some time.) If your oven dial or digital-LED tells you that this oven heats to 350 °C, check this out on the thermometer. If it falls short or goes over, then you know you must compensate in all your temperature readings. For instance, if the temperature gauge only goes to 330 °C rather than 350 °C, you know that your oven will always bake 20 °C cooler than what the temperature says on the dial and you would therefore compensate with more time.

Know your oven

Different ovens cook in different ways. If you are writing a cookbook, and say, you only have an Aga, you will need to test your recipes on a normal domestic oven, either gas or electric. You may have to go to someone else's house to do that.

If you are a professional chef, you need to consider that the home cook will not have access to efficient and rapid high-heat professional ovens. Recipes need to be tested on a domestic oven.

Oven temperatures

The UK uses Celsius and the United States Fahrenheit. Again, if you have an overseas readership, or would like one, write your oven temperatures in both systems. Learn to convert Celsius to Fahrenheit and vice versa. And don't forget gas marks either. Most cookbooks will have all three. For blogs, people can use online resources to convert the temperatures. But making the effort to write out all three will make your blog look more professional and considered, which is important when you are starting out.

Key idea

Remember to tell people to take things out of the oven once they are cooked. Yes, I know, it seems self-evident, but really recipe writing is an instruction manual. You have to assume that the reader knows nothing. You have to state the obvious.

Test, test, test!

The key to accurate recipe writing is testing. Different recipe writers have different attitudes to testing. Most publishers do not have a budget for testers, unless you are a big star. The likes of me and you have to do our own testing.

While Nigel Slater says: 'I have never been the sort of cook who tests a recipe to death', David Lebowitz explains that, in his case: 'Most recipes are tested at least three times, often more. (Because I am crazy, the *tarte tropézienne* – a cake with four separate components – was tested seventeen times. Do the math – and the dishes – on that one!)'

At the very least, you need to have cooked the recipe once. **Always, always, always** test a recipe. Even if you are adapting a recipe from a cookery book or a highly reputed website, test it yourself. You'd be surprised how many 'official' recipes don't work. Testing will make you a better cook, too. Practice makes perfect.

The best recipes are those that we know backwards and forwards. For instance, my spaghetti napoletana I could actually make with my eyes closed. I've made it literally hundreds of times. I know every shortcut. I know how to make it quicker, how to make it slower. I know how to make it with small cherry tomatoes, with large squashy ones, with tomato purée, with chopped tinned tomatoes. I've pared it down to a few easy steps. I've made it every which way. It's a family standard in my house. But clearly I'm not going to be as practised with every dish. But that's the gold standard. Even here, though, one can easily forget steps when writing down how to make something.

 ## Key idea

For recipe writing, think like a scientist. The more accurate your recipes, the more your readers will trust you.

Copyright

Let's discuss the confusing matter of recipe copyright. Most recipes are not original. Recipes are like Chinese whispers: every time someone cooks them, they turn out slightly differently. You cannot copyright, for instance, a classic recipe such as a Victoria sponge or a recipe for hummus. These dishes are in the canon. All we can do as cooks is slightly tweak them. A 'Vicky sponge' needs certain ingredients in a certain quantity combined and baked in a predetermined order. You can put a different flavour in there, you can add a different fruit, you can make it smaller or bigger, but basically a Victoria sponge is still a Victoria sponge.

Ditto hummus. Hummus needs chickpeas, tahini, salt, lemon and olive oil. You can change the bean. You can change the oil. You can play around with the recipe but hummus is hummus is hummus.

I recently had a problem with recipe copyright. A UK cupcake firm came out with a Marmite cupcake recipe and sold the cakes from multiple outlets. They got an awful lot of publicity for this unusual idea. Trouble is, I first came up with the idea four years previously and I had blogged and photographed it. I also put the recipe in my cookbook *Supper Club: Recipes and Notes from the Underground Restaurant*. So it was a matter of public record that I had first done a Marmite cupcake recipe. Actually, I had done two recipes, one with Marmite caramel and the other with Marmite chocolate.

This cupcake firm had combined my two recipes into one. So, you could say, they changed the recipe enough to make it their own. Unfortunately, they used the exact wording from the method of my recipe. They also used, as a quote from the managing director of the cupcake firm, a line from my blog post.

The problem with copying and pasting someone else's recipe is you often slip up.

Key idea

Note that, legally, ingredients cannot be copyrighted. The method cannot be copyrighted either. Minor changes and rewriting the method is not illegal, although it is not terribly ethical. But words can be copyrighted. If you copy the exact same words in the method of a recipe from someone else, that's a breach of copyright. Using the exact same words in the exact same order from somebody else's blog post, without crediting them, is a breach of copyright.

David Lebowitz, in a fascinating article for the website The Food Blog Alliance, talks about recipe attribution and how to give a polite nod to those who came before (as recipe writers, we are all standing on the shoulders of our predecessors):

'When modifying someone else's recipe, use the phrase "adapted from".

If you change a recipe significantly, you may be able to call it your own. If you have obviously used the original recipe in the development of your version despite the changes then you should use "inspired by".

If three ingredients are changed, you can claim the recipe as your own. This would also require it to be more or less unrecognizable from the original in the method and techniques used.

If in doubt, give credit.'

Food essay writing

Food essays situate food within a context, be it political or ethical. This kind of writing can require investigative reporting. Examples of writers or food broadcasters who work within this genre are Joanna Blythman, Sheila Dillon and Felicity Lawrence. With his book *On Eating Animals*, Jonathan Safran Foer pursues investigations in the field by visiting slaughterhouses and meat factories. So does author Michael Pollan. In the 'Fire' chapter of his 2013 book *Cooked* he visited the pit masters of North Carolina, helped out at a barbecue festival in Manhattan before travelling to the Basque Country to watch the chefs at work in the kitchen of Bittor (Victor) Arguinzoniz. In 2014 *The Guardian* carried out an investigation into chicken processing and the spread of the bug camplyobacter, written and researched by Felicity Lawrence. Stories like these can lead to action by government and this can be very rewarding.

For this type of work it's better to get some journalistic training. You certainly need to find out how to interview people. Many investigations take a long time, even years.

Food news: trends

Most newspapers and magazines like to do a yearly trend piece, particularly in the new year – what's hot and what's not. Usually, journalists will ask various members of the food industry – chefs, suppliers, journalists and bloggers – to comment or give their predictions.

There is a new category of food writer, however, who has emerged over the last few years – the food 'futurologist', someone who predicts what we will be eating in the future. One example is Dr Morgaine Gaye, who maintains a blog, sends out newsletters, gives talks and speeches and is frequently quoted in news and features on the future of food.
Dr Gaye has predicted, for instance, that we will move towards eating more insects.

Travel and food

For me, this is one of the most attractive sectors of food writing –
it's the heady combination of trips abroad and food. It's a kind of
food anthropology, seeking to understand a people, a culture or a
nation via their cuisine. When I visited South Africa, I reported on
unusual African ingredients that people may not know about in the
UK. South Africa is called the 'rainbow nation' due to the varied
peoples that make up that nation, from Dutch Afrikaaners to British
descendants of colonial times, to Cape Malays hailing originally
from Java, to the Indians of Durban, to the various African peoples
such as Zulu or Xhosa. Each has contributed towards the cooking
and food ways of South Africa. You have the history of South Africa
on your plate.

Snapshot exercise

When you go on your trip, think about the following questions.
How does geography and climate shape the diet? What are the
seasons? What are the key ingredients?

Visit markets. Eat in both poor and rich restaurants. Eat street
food.

The place you visit need not be exotic or expensive. You may be
just going to Birmingham to visit a friend. What food is typical of
Birmingham? You might think 'classic British cuisine' but it is more
likely to be a Balti, a particular kind of curry cooked in metal wok-
like dishes.

Food writer Qin Xie writes frequently about food and travel for
various media outlets. She suggests trying in-flight magazines for
this kind of writing, as they pay quite well. Qin Xie also mentions
another method of learning how to cook which combines with travel
journalism: 'One blogger wrote to a top Italian cookery school and
offered to blog every day if she could attend for free. They agreed.'
Knowing a destination is really important, Qin Xie says. You need
to have good research or have insight into the culture, on a deeper
level than just a tourist.

Geeky food writing

Most cookbooks, food columns and food blogs are aimed at the home cook, containing fairly simple recipes that he or she could rustle up in a short amount of time. But there is another type of writing for the very serious cook. It's not so much the complex classic French cookery of professional chefs or, say, *kaiseki*, classic Japanese cookery, but a scientific approach to food whereby it might take days to make a dish. For this kind of food writing and testing, you may need specialist equipment such as a sous-vide machine. You may need ingredients that are difficult to find; perhaps you may even have to grow them yourself. This category also encompasses the DIY food movement, whereby people are canning (or bottling) their own food, or curing their own salami, or dehydrating vegetables.

Authors such as Harold McGee in the United States and Dr Peter Barham in the United Kingdom have advanced this kind of food writing, explaining to the layperson as well as to the would-be 'molecular chef' the scientific basis of food preparation. As Dr Barham says: 'Understanding the chemistry and physics of cooking should lead to improvements in performance in the kitchen.' This is no Jamie's 30-minute meal making; this is serious stuff, for the geek.

An example of this kind of highly technical, slightly obscure food genre is the blog 'Ideas in food', run by a Japanese/American couple, Aki Kamozawa and H. Alexander Talbot. One day they are making a shake from seafood (!), the next they are making flour from dehydrated kimchi. It's weird but fascinating. These guys are literally inventing new foods.

American food activist Sandor Ellix Katz also comes under this category, in that his 'recipes' often take weeks. He advocates fermented foods such as sauerkraut, both as a health benefit and also because fermenting boosts flavour. The sixth taste *umami* ('savouriness'), discovered by a Japanese scientist, is present in all fermented foods such as Marmite, coffee, chocolate, soy sauce, sourdough and cheese. Katz has revolutionized the thinking in food circles about fermentation, although his style is folksy rather than scientific. He prefers to let nature do the work, letting natural processes break down vegetables with a little salt, for example, or making 'live' sauerkraut brimming with probiotics. He's been called the 'rock star of micro-organisms' (by me, probably) and his work has been hugely influential in a culture obsessed with sell-by dates.

The behemoth book in this genre is Nathan Myhrvold's *Modernist Cuisine* (2011), a four-volume magnum opus that cost £600 when it came out. (I think the paperback version now sells for about £250.) Featuring incredible photography, these volumes sum up 'modernist' cookery, also known as 'molecular cuisine'. If you are a scientist or a serious cook, this may be the direction you want to go in.

Health and diet writing

This is big business so don't neglect it as a possibility for your chosen field of writing. Categories include all the 'free from' diets such as gluten-free, lactose-free, wheat-free, Palaeolithic, low-GI, high-fibre and low-fat. There is always a diet book in the top ten bestsellers list. Obesity in Western countries is becoming a tremendous problem. One of my more popular blog posts was called 'The Renal Diet', in which I worked with a charity connected with a renal dialysis ward in an East London hospital. I interviewed the patients, who have very restricted low-salt and low-liquid diets, and tried to come up with some interesting recipes.

Increasingly, publishers are catering to specialist diets. Katy Salter, whom I interviewed for the pitching tips in Chapter 9, became aware in recent years that her health was suffering due to a dairy allergy. She has now written *Dairy-free Delicious* (Quadrille, 2015). Gluten-free or wheat-free diets are very popular to the point that, while only 1 in 100 people in the UK are coeliac, many people believe that cutting down on gluten will benefit their health. This is an area where food writers can specialize.

Wine and other drinks writing

Don't forget we drink as well as eat! Obviously, wine writing is a well-known category of expertise. Having done a Level 2 WSET (Wine & Spirit Education Trust) qualification, which was fascinating, I would recommend getting a little training in this field. But, ultimately, tasting and knowing what you like is all you need.

While Fiona Beckett writes about both food and wine, it is her wine expertise that marks her out from the rest. She writes a wine column for *The Guardian* and has a successful blog – matchingfoodandwine.com.

Qin Xie, who wants to specialize in sweet wines after taking her advanced WSET course, says that the wine world is very generous with information. 'Wine writers still like each other, like it was with the early days of food blogging,' she remarks ruefully, comparing the relative competitiveness between wine writers/bloggers and food writers/bloggers.

Helen McGinn, who writes the award-winning and witty blog theknackeredmotherswineclub.com, has a professional wine background, having worked as a wine buyer for a big supermarket chain before quitting to bring up her children. She's now got a new career: her book *The Knackered Mother's Wine Club* (Macmillan, 2013) became a bestseller, she writes a wine column for the *Daily Mail* and she is a regular guest on the *Alan Titchmarsh Show*.

So stardom, or at least regular work, could lie at the bottom of a glass.

Speciality/industry/trade press food writing

Don't sneer – these can be great gigs. I first met Anna Sbuttoni, the 'Citrus Correspondent' of *Fresh Produce Journal* (one of the UKs oldest magazines, going since 1895), on a trip to South Africa to visit grapefruit farmers. Her job sounded, on the face of it, to be fairly mundane, but in reality she spends her whole time travelling to exotic countries. Sure, she has to spend an unnatural amount of time talking to big-booted farmers, wandering around seemingly identical orchards of fruit, and visiting multiple packing plants, but each time she gets to experience a new country, have some nice meals out, and maybe even go for an elephant ride in a safari park. Anna's career has gone very well: she is now working for the UK Food Channel as digital editor.

Stefan Chomka, *Restaurant* magazine deputy editor

'The trade press pays better, it's an easier route and is less likely to be based in London.'

Magazines such as *The Caterer* and *The Grocer* and sites like bighospitality.co.uk which talk about the industry behind the scenes are hugely influential in the food industry, in a way that the consumer press isn't. I once had a large piece on my underground farmers' market in *The Grocer*, which is taken by every supermarket, restaurant and bar in the country, and what surprised me was that I got so much more feedback and many more emails from that piece than I would from an equivalent article in a national newspaper.

Food history

This is another important genre in food writing. This requires research and time and reading. Some of the writers will also translate, test and update old recipes. Ivan Day, probably one of the best-known British food history writers, is frequently asked to talk about his subject on TV and radio.

Regula Llewin is a Belgian blogger known as Miss Foodwise. She is crazy about British food and culture, particularly British historical recipes. Her profession as a graphic designer and the well-styled photography on her blog have helped her win several blogging awards and she has been shortlisted for the Saveur Blogging Awards.

Key idea

Remember that writing about food is not just about restaurant reviewing or writing cookery books and recipes. There are many roads to pursue in order to have a career in food writing.

We are going to look at the history of food writing – where we've been. For, as Shakespeare said, 'What is past is prologue.'

4

A short history of food writing

Writers have always included food in their writing: banquets, hummus, wine, fish and loaves are mentioned in the Bible, for instance. Food is one of the most accessible subjects, for everybody eats at least three times a day. Food writers sometimes write about not eating, as in diet books. Whatever, when it comes to basic functions, food is more easily obtained than sex, and is a more popular subject than sleep. Here is a brief history. Do try to read some of the writers mentioned – it means you can dip into their texts and recipes and quote from them. Regard this whole chapter as homework, as an extended reading list.

Today there are, of course, hundreds of food writers but the authors I have selected are chosen for the quality of their prose and the fact that they have advanced the ongoing conversation about food, rather than for their brand name, their restaurant, the photography and art direction of their books, or for their television fame.

Overview

From the Middle Ages onwards, cookbooks were often household compendiums or directions for servants. They tended to talk about the aristocratic diet and lifestyle; archaeological digs have often revealed more about the common diet. Much later, in the twentieth century, cookbooks were designed for women without servants or cooks, to be used as instruction manuals.

Today, although many people do not know how to cook even basic recipes, cookbooks are no longer manuals; they are coffee table or gift books, and visually stunning. This is the only way to compete with free recipes on the Internet, TV shows and YouTube videos. Cookbooks by top chefs such as René Redzepi of Noma, Heston Blumenthal of the Fat Duck, or Magnus Nilssen of Faviken are not really designed for the home cook at all, many of the ingredients being impossible to obtain (although this is improving with online shopping), or necessitating techniques that require specialist equipment. Magnus Nilssen, for instance, has a recipe for birch butter, whereby you must slowly char a log of birch wood then store your freshly churned butter made from scratch within the hollow of the log and store it for 18 months. I can't see the average housewife preparing this of an evening for the kids' tea. But it's fun and inspirational to find out about. These books are merely starting points, the fine-dining equivalent of haute couture designs that will eventually filter down, infinitely simplified, to the local supermarket, and then to the home cook. Still, in a world where only 12 per cent of the population (specifically, in the UK) have ever bought an avocado, the food writer must be realistic as to what the home cook will attempt.

Since the advent of mass tourism in the 1960s, people are influenced by food they have eaten on holiday, a time when we tend to eat at restaurants more frequently. Tourists return home and, partly in pursuit of happy memories while abroad, hope to recreate the same meal. This had led to almost every nationality's cuisine being represented through cookbooks. Every country has their resident Italian, Spanish, French, Indian, Chinese cookbook expert and cookbook writer to translate the ingredients and methods for the native population.

Nowadays, you can add the food of Middle Eastern, Mexican, Vietnamese and Scandinavian cultures to that list. If you come from an ethnic background, this is a great starting point for your writing. Ken Hom did this for the British with Chinese cookery; Madhur Jaffrey popularized Indian cooking in much the same way. Recently, Signe Johansen, of Norwegian parentage, has inspired British cooks to attempt cinnamon buns and home-made gravlax through her books on Scandinavian food and baking, while Sabrina Ghayour, author of the hugely successful *Persiana*, whose parents hail from Iran, is opening the oven door on Persian cookery delights such as crusty rice and rose-petal-dusted lamb chops.

A food writing timeline

GREEKS AND ROMANS

Fourth century BC Archestratus, a Greek poet, writes a poem on wine, appetizers and fish.

400 BC Marcus Gavius Apicius of Rome writes *De re coquinaria* (On Cooking), including a good recipe for early Roman hamburgers.

300–400 BC Lynceus of Samos writes about shopping for food.

234–149 BC Cato the Elder writes about farming and food in *De agri cultura*.

192 BC Athenaeus, a Greek living in Egypt, writes about the Greek banquet in the work known as the *Deipnosophistae*.

100 BC Timachidas of Rhodes writes on dinners and Greek wine and bemoans the advent of big agribusiness in the Roman Empire.

66 BC Petronius writes the *Satyricon*, which recounts the table talk and outrageous banquet held by a nouveau riche former slave.

AD 50 Columella, a Roman living in Spain, writes *De re rustica*, a recipe book with information on preserving and pickling.

THE MIDDLE AGES

c.1300 Guillaume Tirel, a French court chef, writes *The Viandier of Taillevent* including recipes for peacock and apple tart.

1350 In Germany the cookbook *Buoch von guoter Spise* (Book of Good Eating) is published as part of the 'house book' for Michael of Leone.

1390 In England, the royal chefs of Richard II publish *A Form of Cury* (from the French *cuire* – 'to cook', not 'curry').

FRANCE

1806 Grimod de la Reynière, perhaps the first restaurant critic, publishes *L'Almanach des gourmands*, an annual guide to the new fangled post-French Revolution invention of the restaurant. He also started a delicatessen in Lyon.

1825 Jean Anthelme Brillat-Savarin writes *La Physiologie du goût* (The Physiology of Taste) and comes up with one of the most famous food aphorisms of all time: 'Tell me what you eat and I'll tell you what you are.'

1833 Publication of Marie-Antoine Carême's *L'Art de la cuisine française*. Probably the first celebrity chef, Carême specializes in *pièces-montées* (elaborate gastronomic centrepieces), classifies the 'mother sauces' and is a big fan of skewers.

1903 Georges Auguste Escoffier, chef and writer, writes *Le Guide culinaire*, and updates Carême's recipes. He invents two dishes named after the opera singer Dame Nellie Melba: Peach Melba and Melba Toast.

BRITAIN

1747 Hannah Glasse writes *The Art of Cookery*. Many great British cookery books are written by household cooks rather than restaurant chefs. Hannah Glasse was the first and greatest.

1806 Mrs Rundell writes *A New System of Domestic Cookery*, one of the cookbooks used by Jane Austen and hugely popular in America.

1836 Mrs Beeton, journalist and 'career woman' who didn't actually have much time to cook, writes the bestseller *Mrs Beeton's Book of Household Management*. Many of her recipes are plagiarized from Eliza Acton and other cookbook authors. Mrs Beeton became very famous, but she lived to only 28 years old.

1845 Eliza Acton writes *Modern Cookery for Private Families*. She introduces the idea of listing the ingredients at the beginning of recipes and saying how long it would take to cook.

1932 Publication of *Good Things in England* by Florence White, the first ever freelance food journalist.

1933 Publication of *Good Food on the Aga* by Ambrose Heath.

1950 Elizabeth David, probably the most famous post-war food writer, publishes *Mediterranean Food*, delivering a ray of sunshine into a food culture decimated by rationing.

c.1950 Before Fanny Craddock became the lurid TV cook, she writes food columns and books under the name of 'Bon Viveur'. She is the originator of the prawn cocktail.

1957 Publication of *Plats du jour* by Patience Grey and Primrose Boyd (don't you just love their names?) – similar to Elizabeth David in that they wrote about Mediterranean food.

1968 Claudia Roden, originally from Egypt, publishes *A Book of Middle Eastern Food* (1968). *The Book of Jewish Food* (1997) is another essential classic. Her books can be read as memoir, travelogue and anthropology.

1969 Delia Smith, cook and TV presenter, starts as a recipe columnist for the *Daily Mirror*, and later the *Evening Standard* and later presents simplified cooking courses on TV. Her website is today well known for its tried-and-tested recipes. 'Doing a Delia' became a phrase, meaning you were cooking from one of her books for your dinner party.

1971 Jane Grigson, columnist and author of many books, publishes *Good Food*.

1988 Nigel Slater, a gardener as well as a cook, becomes the food writer for *Marie Claire*. *The Kitchen Diaries* (2005), in which Nigel recounts in diary form every meal he had for a year, and *Appetite* (2000) are two books well worth having on your bookshelf. Slater writes simple, creative recipes for the home cook.

1991 Prue Leith, restaurateur and cookery school founder, publishes *Leith's Cookery Bible*.

1998 Nigella Lawson publishes *How to Eat* (1998), followed by *How to be a Domestic Goddess* (2000), probably her most important books. Her recipes are simple and un-cheffy. She kickstarts the retro baking cult among modern women, which reaches its apogee with *The Great British Bake Off*.

1999 Hugh Fearnley-Whittingstall publishes the first of the River Cottage cookbooks, encouraging cooks to forage for ingredients. He is well known for his food activism with regards to meat and fish consumption. The River Cottage series, written by Hugh and other authors, covering a variety of subjects from preserving, curing, baking to gardening, are interesting and informative.

2008 Yotam Ottolenghi and Sami Tamimi, chefs and authors, publish *Ottolenghi*, introducing a new palette of foods to the British public, using Middle Eastern ingredients and modern cookery.

THE UNITED STATES

1941 If anybody can be considered to have written food 'literature', as in fine prose, it is Mary Fisher. *Consider the Oyster* (1941) and *Gastronomical Me* (1943) are just two books you should read.

1961 Julia Child, wife of an American diplomat stationed in Paris, publishes, with two French co-authors *Mastering the Art of French Cooking*, introducing America to classic French cookery. The first Hollywood movie featuring bloggers is about an early food blogger, Julie Powell, who wrote a blog called 'The Julie/Julia Project' (2002), where she records her attempt to cook her way through the entirety of Julia Child's most famous cookbook, every day for a year, 524 recipes in total. The movie, called *Julie & Julia* (2009), was directed by one of my favourite 'food' writers, Nora Ephron, who wrote the novel *Heartburn* about a food writer's divorce, in which recipes are cleverly intermingled with the plot.

1984 Harold McGee publishes his seminal *On Food and Cooking: The Science and Lore of the Kitchen* (1984) explaining the process and chemistry behind, for instance, the Maillard reaction (the flavour obtained by browning food). He has been very influential on 'modernist' chefs such as Heston Blumenthal.

1995 Alice Waters, chef and author, pioneered 'localism' (where you eat ingredients grown and reared in your geographic area), 'seasonality' (where you eat food that in season) and organic food (food grown without pesticides). *Chez Panisse Menu Cookbook* (1995), which consists of recipes from her award-winning restaurant and *The Art of Simple Food* (2007) are American classic cookbooks with simple, elegant, doable recipes.

2000 Chef Anthony Bourdain publishes *Kitchen Confidential: Adventures in the Culinary Underbelly* (2000), which is the start of a trend in rock 'n' roll kitchen biographies, portraying the chef as a rebellious, hard-living, drug-fuelled rock star. Every sweaty overworked chef, sous chef and line cook, and every macho food writer has dreamed of emulating Bourdain. The genre has become a bit tired but was like a jolt of electricity when it came out.

2006 Publication of Bill Buford's *Heat: An Amateur's Adventures as Kitchen Slave, Line Cook, Pasta-maker, and Apprentice to a Dante-quoting Butcher in Tuscany* (2006). Buford is not specifically a food writer but his journey as a 40-year-old 'kitchen bitch' in Mario Batali's restaurant is an incredible example of dedicated research. A brilliant read, too.

2006 Publication of food activist and food essayist Michael Pollan's thought-provoking *The Omnivore's Dilemma* (2006), followed by *Food Rules: An Eater's Manual* (2009) and *Cooked* (2013). He criticizes America's large-scale agribusiness and talks about ethics in food such as vegetarianism versus meat eating and the obesity epidemic. His famous aphorism is: 'Eat food. Not too much. Mostly plants.'

2009 Michael Ruhlman, home cook and food writer, publishes *Ratio*. This is followed by *20:20 Techniques, 100 Recipes: A Cook's Manifesto* (2011). Both books are a new look at streamlining cooking.

Write exercise – *Place*

Where do you come from? Are you from the UK/USA? If so, what part? Are your parents or grandparents from another part of the world? Write about the food from your area. It can be something you don't like, or find strange, or it can be a loved dish, something that always reminds you of home.

Write exercise – *Time*

I want you to come up with a memory of a dish that one of your parents or grandparents cooked when you were a child. Write a short introduction, then a recipe.

Workshop

Choose a favourite dish and, using different research methods (including the Internet, food history books, museums, libraries, restaurant menus), discover the earliest version of it and trace the changes to this dish until the present day.

An example: blancmange. What does the name mean? Where does this dish originate from? What were the original ingredients?

Another example: mince pies. Why are they called mince? In what era were they most popular? Is the original recipe similar today? Was there ever meat in mince pies?

Background research allows you to contextualize the subject of your food writing.

Next step

In the next chapter we begin to look more closely at how to write about food.

5

How to write about food

In this chapter we will investigate different approaches to food writing. I will talk about whether we can learn to write. I'll also give some techniques for dealing with 'writer's block'.

One can take several approaches: using diary forms or personal memoirs, providing technical information about recipes and cooking techniques, creative writing approaches, reportage and investigatory methods.

The most important thing is having something to say. If you haven't anything to say, have no opinions about food, about eating, about cooking, about places to eat, then give this book away right now. This book is for the nervous, the unconfident, the feeling all-at-sea and 'where-shall-I-start?' novice, but underneath all that, I'm assuming that you, the reader, is fiercely opinionated about food. You just want a place, a notion, of where to shove it all. And, of course, you want interaction and recognition. Who doesn't?

On writing

I know this is supposed to be a book on food writing. I'm struggling with that because I'm not sure you can teach anyone to write. Don't lose heart, I believe everyone can write; it's just about releasing the voices in your head. So this is the only part of the book, apart from the exercises, where I'll actually say, 'this is how to write'. Why? Because:

1   I'm not a writing teacher.

2   I'm not officially a writer.

To explain:

1 I've taught French, English and cookery. I've never taught writing. The whole idea of a 'writing course' is fairly new. The University of East Anglia started them in the 1980s; local community centres and adult evening classes have writing courses, *The Guardian* run a series of masterclasses led by their journalists. Teaching people how to write is a thriving sector.

2 Not only have I never taught writing, I've never been to a writing class. I've never had lessons. Does that mean I can't write? I can write English. I can fill up pages. My grammar and spelling are OK (I do struggle a bit with apostrophes) and people seem to find my work interesting and entertaining. I just write down all the stuff that's in my head. There's loads of it. I seem to have an opinion on absolutely everything. The act of writing is psychologically useful to me because it clears out some of the head garbage. But I haven't trained to be 'A Writer' – it's not a job title.

It seems writing has become similar to politics in this way. In the old days, politicians were people who lived their lives, got jobs outside of politics, and then, as a result of their experiences in the real world, went into politics to improve society. Today's politicians study politics at university, leave and get a job as a SpAd (special advisor) then become MPs. They never have jobs outside of politics: they study, live and work in their own hermetic society. Many writers today do English degrees, then creative writing courses; then they become writers. This can work but, more importantly to be a writer, you need material, you need a life to draw upon. The best food writing comes from the same place.

The importance of thinking (not to be confused with procrastination)

Every book I write needs at least a few months' thinking. It's almost like getting into a role, Stanislavsky-style method acting. When I wrote my book on vegan food, I went vegan for six months. How else, I felt, could I write about this diet?

Your thinking at the beginning of a project will change as you go along. But do not underestimate the time needed for thinking in advance of writing. This is even more the case if you are on your second book or your second batch of articles for a column or perhaps writing your second year of blog posts. It's similar to the first album of a musician: all the stuff that was stored up for years has found an outlet. The first album was a success, and congratulations, you've had recognition; maybe you are now a rock star, so now you've got to come up with the goods but, this time, to order. It's the famous 'second album' syndrome – what have you got to say next? You don't have years to formulate your thoughts. It can feel like you have run out of ideas, the well has run dry.

This is when you might feel blocked. Here are my unblocking tips which are also useful for just getting started:

- Have a shower. I find flowing water is a big help. I get my best ideas in the shower.
- Write anything. Just fill two pages every single day. Use this as a warm-up. Don't edit.
- Don't go back. Don't even read it.
- Relax. Perfection is the enemy of creativity. Don't think about the end product. (Unless you are on a 'flow day' where everything magically can't stop coming out of your fingertips.)
- Some writers have a routine. I don't. I don't have that kind of discipline. You might read of the likes of Stephen King writing 2,000 words a day no matter what. You may hear of writers that rise at 6 a.m., have one cup of coffee, write until lunch then have the rest of the day off. Don't be intimidated by this.

Your routine, your rhythm, is whatever works for you. It may take a while to find yours or you may never find one. Some writers work in spurts. But I would encourage you, even if it is a tremendous effort, cranking it out without inspiration, to write every day.

- I find I need no distractions. I clear my schedule. I turn down invitations. This is the lonely bit. Sometimes you feel crushingly isolated but then you hit upon a thin vein of gold, keep writing, and then you don't need any other voice than your own. Those moments are exhilarating.

- I find stimulants do help. Coffee. Cigarettes. I'm a non-smoker but the odd one can break your routine and help you concentrate. Maybe it's not the cigarette but doing something illicit that spurs creativity. Most of the great writers took amphetamines or cocaine. But don't fall into a trap of addiction – there is nothing romantic about that.

- Now I do know food and drink writers who like to, shall we say, 'party' but the thing is most food writers would rather eat than do anything else. They'd rather eat than have sex.

But it really boils down to one thing: write. Just write.

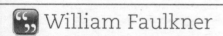 William Faulkner

'Don't be a writer; be writing.'

Writing style

I'm personally not a fan of too much description. I tend to skip all that and just read the dialogue while sucking up the plot. I recognize great writing and beautiful phrasing. I just don't want too much of it. I want story. I want facts. I want emotion. I want opinion. I want experience.

But some writers are known for their elegant way with description. It doesn't have to be long, just a few choice words.

Diane Jacob

'*Food writers tend to use too many adjectives. Read Calvin Trillin. He doesn't use any!*'

Author and *Times* columnist Caitlin Moran is a talented writer though not a food writer. Consider, however, these examples from one article in which she describes family meals as she grew up:

> a) '*Crazed by the idea of making a posset, I persuaded my mother to buy a nutmeg: it was nine-and-a-half pence, and used only on special occasions, carefully grated, to leave perfumed freckles on thickening milk.*'
>
> b) '*All were served, of course, with ketchup – pollocked all over the dish, like vinegary murder.*'
>
> c) '*We would sit on the edge of overgrown well – autumn damp, slow and golden – and rub the bloom of damsons off with our thumbs, while crushing drowsy wasps under our wellington boots.*'

From *The Times Saturday Magazine* (2014)

Her style is observational and detailed, nostalgic but modern. She employs interesting words rarely applied to food such as 'pollocked', 'crazed' and 'murder'. All the senses are there: smell ('perfumed'), sight ('bloom of damsons', 'damp, slow and golden'), touch ('crushing', 'rubbing', 'grated') and sound ('drowsy wasps'). In fact, the one sense Moran doesn't explicitly use is taste. But the atmosphere is so skilfully sketched out with a flick of a pen that we can picture the scene and taste the food.

Styles and techniques

Write

The Guardian's 'Word of Mouth' food articles always start with a fact and finish with a question. Have a look through some examples.

> Next, select a food headline in the news, for instance today I read 'NHS to give bariatric surgery to more people in an effort to stem the increase of diabetes 2'. Using the story as the first opening paragraph, write a short piece, explaining in food terms what this might mean. Should people go on a diet? Should the NHS pay for this? How are people's eating habits making this a problem?
>
> End the piece with a question or several questions.

Why end a blog post with a question?

Because you want a response; you want readers to comment with their own experiences. The popularity of many online articles is judged by comments, shares and tweets (RTs).

Writing proper English

You don't have to write university-level English; in fact, that can be quite dull, but you do have to have a voice. This voice is not necessarily conventionally 'well-educated' with a large sophisticated vocabulary. This voice can be poorly educated 'white trash' as in Ernest Mathew Mickler's best-selling cookbook *White Trash Cooking*. Here are some examples of his writing:

> *'I know you'll lay down and scream when you taste Loretta's Chicken Delight and Tutti's Fruited Porkettes are fit for the table of a queen. Just how can you miss with a dessert that calls for twenty-three Ritz crackers?'*
> *'It's not hard to catch on to our ways. Even an awful cook will soon sop them up and become deathly accurate with the sweet potato opines and Miss Bill's Bucket Dumplings.'*

In a recipe there are instructions like the following for Baked Sweet Potato:

> *'Select plump, smooth potatoes. Wash 'em and grease 'em.'*

Fantastic, no? You can hear Betty Sue or whichever 'white trash' housewife talking, you can picture her cooking, her house, her kitchen.

amateurgourmet.com

'Nothing saddens me more in food writing (and I'm sometimes guilty of it myself) than a person who feels obliged to force adjectives that are completely unnatural: "The wine was gingery, with a hint of spruce, aflutter with the sad poetry of a summer's day." Don't be pretentious! Don't write the way you think you should write, just write in your NORMAL voice. A clear, compelling voice is essential for any kind of writing success.'

Bee Wilson, daughter of historian A.N. Wilson, writes for *The Telegraph*. In her book *Consider the Fork* (2013), she writes in a scholarly, well-researched but also very accessible style about kitchen equipment through the ages:

'A wooden spoon – most trusty and lovable of kitchen implements – looks like the opposite of "technology", as the word is normally understood. It does not switch on and off or make funny noises. It has no patent or guarantee. There is nothing futuristic or shiny or clever about it.'

Write exercise

Use an item from your kitchen as a starting point for inspiration. For example:

A colander. Think about its form, the material it's made from, its colour, its use, how long it's been around for. Is it a necessity in the kitchen? Write a short piece about it, getting inspiration from the quote from Bee Wilson's book above. (*350 words*)

Workshop

Write a short restaurant review. Make sure that you use all the senses:

Sight: colour, hue, light, form. Is the restaurant dimly lit? What colour is that stuffed patty pan courgette? What shape is the quinoa? How would you describe it?

Hearing: the murmurs of the restaurant, the spitting of the fat in the pan, the stallholders of the market shouting in the old square.

Smell: the taco stall that pongs of tripe; the odour of cinnamon, butter and yeast filling the restaurant.

Touch: is it smooth? Is it shiny? Is it soft? Is the menu sticky? Are the seats made from chamois leather?

Taste: obviously for food, this is essential. It's probably the hardest part – how do you describe how something tastes without resorting to cliché? Think of the basic tastes – salt, sweet, sour, bitter. Describe the temperature, describe the spices, describe the mouth feel. Use analogies from music or art or politics.

(500 words)

Interviews and taking a journalistic approach

Interviews are a great way to get information about a person or subject. This can range from interviewing a chef or, for example, interviewing food writers for this book!

Try to establish before the interview how much time the subject will have to speak to you. This will give you an idea of the pace of the interview. If the subject has only 15 minutes, you are going to have to get to the core of what you want to know very quickly.

Research. Don't go into an interview without being prepared. Know who the subject is and what they do beforehand.

Be informed about their work. Read their work if they've written a book or articles. Eat their food if they are a chef. Go in with a measure of knowledge.

Find out your own stuff – don't depend on Wikipedia.

Ask direct, simple questions. The questions can be boiled down to: Who? What? Why? Where? When?

The most important thing about doing an interview is to listen. Remember to listen. Sometimes the most interesting information is when your interviewee goes off-message and stops promoting the thing they are there to promote. If you aren't listening, you'll miss this opportunity.

If you don't know shorthand (which is advantageous as it means the subject probably cannot read what you are writing down), then record the interview on your phone. Alternatively, learn to write really quickly. The disadvantage of recording is you then have the laborious task of transcribing the interview. So it's best to record *and* write things down. That way you have both things: proof in the recording that they said what you say they said and, secondly, notes where you can focus on what quotes stood out in the interview. Legally, you must inform the interviewee if they are being recorded.

> ## Write exercise
>
> Interview a chef. Ask in a local restaurant. It doesn't have to be a posh restaurant, it doesn't have to be a Michelin-starred chef; it can be a fast-food cook. Ask the questions and find out about their background, why they are doing the job. Find out about their daily schedule from morning to night. Write it up. (*500 words*)

Finding your voice

How to find your voice in writing is something difficult to convey. It emerges from repetition, from practice. The process verges on the spiritual, what Stevie Wonder would call 'Innervisions', and comes from a place of confidence, of being truly yourself. This tends to apply most to creative food writing, but even in reportage and journalism one can distinguish the writer's voice. Write whatever comes out. The more you write, the more that elusive voice will reveal itself. Stuff comes through that you aren't aware of. In fact, one of the joys of writing is that you discover your true self.

A lot of writing is about confidence, feeling that you have the right to express your feelings and assuming that notion called 'literary authority'.

 Key idea

The bottom line is that what all of the writing books, all of the courses, all the university education really do give people is confidence. It can't tell them how to actually write.

Truthfulness, finding one's core self, is an aid to good writing, but this does not mean that the story, the narrative, cannot be semi-fictitious. Like telling a great anecdote, one can rearrange events and conversations so that they have a story arc, so that they are funny and have a punch line.

For example, I visited a place in Colombia called Mompos, which is an island in the middle of a wide river. I stayed in a guesthouse that had two parrots. The parrots talked: one said 'Viva el partido liberal' and the other said 'Viva el partido conservador'. They were political parrots who 'supported' opposing parties. Nobel Prize-winning author Gabriel García Márquez wrote within a genre of fiction called 'magical realism'. People thought he was making stuff up. One of his most famous novels, *One Hundred Years of Solitude* (1967), talks about an island in the middle of a river. Sound familiar? García Márquez spent time on the island of Mompos. Another of his novels, *Love in the Time of Cholera* (1985), tells of political parrots who, yes, spouted those very same slogans. His novels weren't fiction; they were fact. Life is stranger than fiction.

Humour is important. What is it? I once heard someone describe it as a yes/no conflict. Your mind says, 'Yes that works ... no it doesn't' very quickly in an almost infinitesimal moment, and that clash produces laughter. If you enjoy writing it, people enjoy reading it. If you laugh while you are reading your own work, that's a good indicator.

But sometimes writing is hard work and just feels like graft. You have to work through that. Sometimes you write it over a cup of tea and sometimes it's a labour of love and no one reads it. Some people have a free flow – they write organically. But this doesn't always happen and you cannot rely on it.

Use your pain. Some of my best pieces have been written when I feel very hurt or upset by something. Write it all down. Don't press publish. Go back the next day.

Key idea

Write every day. Just think: if you write for two hours a day for a year, you will have a book. When writing a book, don't waste too much time blogging. Blogging is great for getting started. It's a sketchbook where you practise.

Key idea

Fact-check! Don't assume, check. Don't rely on Wikipedia either.

Snapshot exercise

What are you really trying to say? Can you sum up your piece in one sentence? Imagine your piece was an elevator pitch and you had to pitch it to a Hollywood producer in the time that it took to reach the destination floor.

Write exercise

Write about an accident in the kitchen. Write it dramatically.

Edit exercise

Write about the same incident but make it sexy. Yes, introduce a sex scene. This might be terrifying but do it anyway. It'll help you loosen up. Play with your writing.

Structuring a piece

Most articles, like plays, are tripartite: introduction, main body, conclusion.

Here are some basic rules of writing, some inspired by George Orwell's own rules:

1 Never use a metaphor, simile or other figure of speech which you are used to seeing in print.

2 Try to avoid clichés.

3 Check your grammar and punctuation. Many spellcheck programs use American spelling. Make sure, if you are British, that you use British spelling.

4 Try to avoid repetition, although don't get too phobic about this. Use a thesaurus if you get stuck. On the other hand, repetition can be useful when used anaphorically (anaphora is the repetition of a word or phrase at the beginning of successive clauses for rhetorical purposes – Martin Luther King's 'I have a dream' speech provides a famous instance of this).

5 Stick to the same tense – don't jump around. 'Bill was watching TV when he decides to drink a beer' should be 'Bill was watching TV when he decided to drink a beer.'

6 Avoid tautology, which is where you say the same thing twice in different ways (e.g. 'He wrote an autobiography of his own life').

7 Never use a long word where a short one will do (e.g. replace 'analogous' with 'similar').

8 Never use a foreign phrase, a scientific word or jargon if you can think of an everyday English equivalent. This is similar to the above commandment in that words with a Latin root are often longer than the plain Anglo-Saxon version. Avoid jargon because it is exclusive. You want everyone to understand your writing.

9 If it is possible to cut a word out, do so.

10 Never use the passive where you can use the active tense (e.g. *active:* 'Julia washes the dishes'; *passive:* 'The dishes are washed by Julia').

11 Avoid using too many clauses in a sentence.

12 Feel free to break these rules, especially if you are making a joke.

Next step

In the next chapter you'll learn how to set up and write a blog.

6

Blogging about food

In this chapter, I'm going to give you a few technical basics to get you started. I will also talk about creating a good-looking blog because design is incredibly important when trying to attract readers.

I'm going to offer the expertise of successful bloggers.

I'm going to discuss the different types of food blog.

Finally, and most crucially, I'm going to tell you how to get your food blog noticed and read.

Why blog?

Realistically, the most accessible way of getting into food writing is to start a blog. Print journalism is a shrinking industry: newspapers and magazines are downsizing, cutting staff and, increasingly, not paying writers at all. When you see an article by a celebrity chef, perhaps plugging a show or a book or a restaurant or an article with recipes from a recent cookbook, it's most likely to be free content for the newspaper.

Blogs are simultaneously the cause of this situation and the way out of it. You can't buck a trend. Online is the way to go unless you are talking niche, high-concept material that a small dedicated band of subscribers will continue to buy.

It is important to recognize that there are advantages to blogging that journalism does not provide. Blogging, for one thing, is (or used to be) based on a quality known as 'social trust'. Bloggers are trusted as peers. In 2012 I went on a blogging trip to Israel, all expenses paid for seven days. There were no print journalists. When I asked the organizer of the trip why she had invited only bloggers, she said that their research had shown that bloggers have a particular influence, over and above that of journalists or celebrities. Bloggers are seen as friends, as equals.

However, since I started blogging in 2007/8, blogging has become the creature of the PR industry rather than the revolutionary publishing tool that it had the potential to become. I say 'revolutionary' because writing and journalism tend to be the preserve of the rich and connected. Even today, you will see that most journalists have an Oxbridge and/or public school background. Sadly, since the euphoric post-war breakthrough of working-class and other divergent voices on the cultural scene, there has been a backlash. We are back to the days of Eton-educated Prime Ministers, Oxbridge rock bands and public school actors. Which is fine, but where is everyone else? Where are the 'ordinary' (but not ordinary voices) of the rest of us?

Blogging provides this opportunity. You don't need permission. You don't need money. You don't need a degree. You don't need to know anybody. You just do it. All you need is access to a computer and the Internet.

Oh, of course, nowadays, as blogging has progressed to the mainstream, the society girls and boys with the means to employ a professional graphic designer and an Search Engine Optimization (SEO) expert, use expensive cameras, and have the entrepreneurial confidence that comes with private education and a PR budget to push their blog, will still get more exposure than you, the woman or man on the street. Nonetheless, good content will out. Your voice. Your unique song. Sing it.

A brief history of blogging

The word 'blog' comes from 'weblog' and is in origin a form of digital diary. Note that the word 'blog' means the site where you blog. Each entry is a blog post. Sometimes people say to me, 'Oh I loved your blog on so and so.' What they mean is, 'I loved your post on so and so.'

The blogging platform Live Journal started in 1999 but has now shut down. Blogger started in 1999 but was purchased by Google in 2003. WordPress started in 2003, as an offshoot of an earlier model, 'cafe log'. It is now the most popular blogging platform.

Search engines enabled people to look for subjects they were interested in. Blog rolls enabled communities to find each other, as well as permalinks and deep linking. A permalink will generally take you to a home page. Deep links and hyperlinking take you to a specific page. Soon photography was enabled on blogs. Picasa, for instance, encouraged this and was bought by Google in 2004.

Today there are 158 million blogs with a million new blog posts every day. Obviously, only a small proportion of these are related to food.

Key idea

Your online writing is a portfolio, a shop window for your writing skills.

The basics

PICK A NAME

You need to choose a name for your food blog. Make sure it is catchy, short, memorable and easy to spell. This will be your brand. You should use the same name for Twitter and all your other social media. You want a short name or a name that can be easily shortened because, on Twitter, you have only 140 characters per tweet and a long name will take up some of this.

PLATFORMS

As mentioned above, there are two main blogging platforms, Blogger (owned by Google) and WordPress, plus a few others.

Blogger

This is the simplest for the beginner; it's also free. You can set it up in minutes with a gmail.com address. It has simple layouts and the widgets are accessible. I've also heard that, because blogger is part of Google, it will favour a Blogger blog on their search engine.

My blog started on Blogger. But I'm considering transferring to WordPress which is independent and specially built for bloggers.

WordPress

This platform is complex and sophisticated. There are more plug-ins/widgets (extra features to add to your blog), such as a cut-out-and-print-recipe feature, plus SEO help. Search Engine Optimization is a way of nudging search engines to promote your blog posts, which means more readers. I will expand on this later.

On WordPress you can self-host (WordPress.org) or the platform can host the site for you (WordPress.com). Ultimately, you want to be self-hosting. This means that if your blog becomes incredibly popular, it will be able to cope with a large volume of readers.

Let's compare the two. With WordPress.org you will need to buy a domain, which costs about £10 a year. I use 1&1.co.uk. You need to find a domain name that is exclusive to you. You can buy it as a '.com', a '.co.uk', and several other options. Always buy the .com if you can, as this is international.

There are three options with WordPress.com: Basic (free), Premium and Business. The latter two options have more features and cost money, from £99 to £299 annually.

Other platforms

- **Squarespace** Designers particularly like this platform thanks to its clean look. Like WordPress, it has a three-tier pricing structure.
- **Wix** Another simple website builder.
- **Tumblr** This works slightly differently in that, as well as writing your own posts, you reblog other people's posts. Popularity is gained by the amount of times that your post is reblogged or liked. Tumblr has a young demographic, people like my 21-year-old daughter, students and teenagers. It is more visually based, especially 'GIFs', which are like repetitive loops of short sections of film. Buzzfeed has in some ways replicated the Tumblr style. Tumblr, like Reddit (a comment-driven forum), builds 'memes'. (A meme is sort of an in-joke.) Tumblr has a specific vocabulary, developed by users, associated with fandoms (fan bases) and social justice politics. There is not much food on Tumblr but, if you are a teenager, this might be the one for you. Tumblr blogs (or Tumblrs) that feature food are very narrowly focused on one food variety, such as pasta or vegan food. Tumblr, perhaps as a result of the very young audience, also has a worrying abundance of 'thinspiration' or 'pro-ana' (pro-anorexic) blogs – diet and 'health' blogs in which being thin is the main goal.

GOOGLE TOOLS

Once you have set up your blog, there are various Google tools you can use, such as **Google Analytics**. This tells you how many people look at your blog, which posts are most popular, how long they stay on the page and where they come from. **Feedburner** is also owned by Google: it allows you to automatically send your blog posts via a RSS (Rich Site Summary) feed to subscribers, Twitter and Facebook.

FREQUENCY

Do post a certain number of times per month. Cook Sister, one of the earliest food bloggers in the UK, blogs three times a week: Thursday, Saturday and Sunday including a recipe, a review and a 'Saturday snapshot', usually a travel/food photograph. She's absolutely ritualistic about this. This has advantages as your audience know exactly when to check your blog for updates.

Other bloggers are more random.

Legend has it that you shouldn't post on the weekend; instead, post when people are bored at work and want to read your blog.

I tend to blog every four days, except when I'm writing a book (like this one).

MissFoodwise5 blogs just once a month, but each blog post is beautifully styled, photographed and researched, so she is going for quality rather than quantity. If you do blog rarely, it really has to be good to keep your audience. Or, as blogger Chris Pople says, 'If you aren't very good, blog frequently to get your reader figures up.'

 ## Key idea

Aim to blog at least once a week. No three-month gaps and then an apologetic post. Boring. No one cares.

EDITORIAL CONTROL

Spellcheck and grammar check your work. It's easier to make mistakes on a computer screen and, of course, you don't have an editor to prevent you looking sloppy. If it helps, print out your work, proofread it from the hard copy, then correct and publish.

Check that your links work.

Do your research and make sure the facts in your post are correct. If you are unsure, then ask the reader. Say something like: 'This is my experience, what has yours been?' Remember that blogging is a two-way experience: you aren't just broadcasting your opinions; you are sharing. It's a very different attitude to food columnists in the 'dead tree press' where they can talk to the reader from on high, making airy pronouncements. No, blogging is where you are down in the mosh pit with the readers, thrashing it out together, pogoing and sometimes spitting. Blogging is punk and DIY.

Don't write about things you haven't experienced. Write about food you have eaten/cooked, events/restaurants you have visited. This will give your blog authenticity.

Key idea

It helps to think of your blog as a second version of you. It represents you in the world. It's your digital doppelgänger.

COMMENTS

I would recommend that, in the early days as a new blogger, you comment on lots of other blogs. This is an effective way of being noticed and gaining readership. The established bloggers may think you are sucking up too much but it's still worth doing. Everybody likes attention and compliments.

Do reply to commenters. Not only does this up your comment tally, but if someone has made the effort to comment on your blog, it's only courtesy to reply. This ensures a dialogue is created, which encourages commenters and establishes a rapport.

If you get a lot of comments, then respond to them in groups. David Lebowitz does this: he gets so many comments, it would take him all day to reply to each one, so he'll reply every 20 comments. If you don't get many, reply to each one. People are more likely to read a post if it has lots of comments – it shows that it is popular.

Nowadays, people comment less. Often, they will just tweet you what they think about a post, so don't worry too much if you don't get comments. Commenting is less significant today than it was five years ago.

Try to make commenting as easy as possible. Spam comments can be a problem but Blogger, for instance, is doing a better job nowadays of making sure you don't get too much spam.

Key idea

You want to control spam while making commenting easy.

I would advise against having a Captcha filter, where you have to spell a given word to prove you are human. Don't ask readers to log in either. I've heard that Disqus commenting is a great method to use.

Another term to remember is 'sock puppet'. These are people who comment under false identities, usually to create havoc and mischief. Another word for this is 'trolling' – getting a rise out of the writer or the other commenters for some strange thrill. Trolls don't believe what they are writing. There has been much discussion over the last couple of years about how women writers/bloggers receive worse trolling and online abuse than men do. There have been cases where prominent women such as Caroline Criado Perez, a writer and campaigner (she successfully lobbied to get a woman pictured on British paper money, other than The Queen of course), were threatened with violence on Twitter. The culprits turned out to be an alcoholic woman and a loner man, really quite sad people. While it is true that women are targeted far more than men, I also think it is important to maintain a sense of perspective. If a troll had a happy fulfilled life, they wouldn't be trolling.

If you get the odd negative comment, please take a robust attitude. I publish all negative comments. Why? Well, I think that's more fun to read than a whole series of 'we think you are fabulous' comments. It's good to have a little stirring up of debate. But I must say, I've been lucky, I haven't had a whole lot of negative comments. You can also choose to moderate all comments prior to publishing and delete any comments you deem offensive or unhelpful to the debate. Naturally, the more controversial your subject matter, the more likely it is you are going to receive contentious comments. Try not to take it personally. If you do get an abusive and threatening commenter who implies they are going to take violent action, report it to the police. They can find out the IP address and put a halt to it.

SHARING

Make sure that you have sharing buttons on every post. If possible, get these buttons designed to match your blog. Sharing your blog posts with Twitter, Facebook, Pinterest and any other social media is a great way to boost traffic.

ETHICS AND THE LAW

Disclosure

It is the law that, if you do a restaurant review that you attended as a guest, or if you mention a product that you got for free, then you must state that you got it for free.

Key idea

Again to repeat: you must declare that you've received a 'freebie'. Yes, this is the law.

Cookies

You are supposed to have a cookies disclaimer on your blog, asking readers for their permission to use cookies. This is EU law since 2011, introduced because of concern about security. Cookies are a way for sites to remember whether you have visited them before.

A cookie is a small bit of data that gets stored in your computer. It can be useful – it remembers whether you were in the process of buying something from that website and had something in the basket, or it remembers your password for that site, or your buying history.

It can also remember your browsing history, the last time you visited. Cookies also enable targeted advertising. Have you seen many weight-loss adverts on your Facebook page recently? It's annoying, isn't it? This is the result of targeted advertising – if you are a foodie, it's likely that if you mention food in your communication the Facebook cookies will assume that you want to lose weight.

Licensing

Be careful of licensing. For instance, you can't create a Harry Potter cupcake. The licence belongs to Warner Brothers and J.K. Rowling. Events like the London 2012 Olympics were very tightly licensed so be careful if you ever create recipes around an event. I fell foul of this. In 2010 I decided to do a Harry Potter-themed supper club at Halloween. Just one week beforehand, I got a letter from Warner Brothers lawyers saying I was not allowed to include 'Harry Potter' in the name of the supper club night. I was also not allowed to serve butterbeer. I tweeted this. This story went around the world, which was great publicity for me and my blog. I wasn't making a habit of hosting Harry Potter nights and it wasn't intentional. I could understand if I was opening up a full-time restaurant serving Harry Potter-themed food but this was a one-off.

However, copyright and trademark lawyers have to fight from the off because, if they are deemed to have been lax, then it may be construed that the copyright isn't important to the client.

TAGS AND KEYWORDS

When you tag posts, try to use no more than five tags (in Blogger these are called 'labels'). Tags are descriptions of the post or the blog that sum up the subject matter. Keep it simple: if you post mostly vegetarian recipes, tag the recipe 'vegetarian'. If you are a recipe blog, tag the post 'recipe'. Tagging enables search engines to further categorize your blog. Try to link to the product, book, event or restaurant in the first paragraph of your blog post. Include the subject of your blog post in bold in the first paragraph. This will help search engines find you.

LINKING

'Follow' and 'no-follow' links

'Follow' links, which helped boost your site's page rank within Google, were abused by SEO managers. It meant that comments became spam, in the hope that you'd publish them, complete with a 'follow link', to another site. To combat this abuse, 'no-follow' links were invented. These mean that you can link to another site but effectively you are saying to search engines, in the words of an SEO expert, 'Don't give this link juice' – that is, don't give it extra search engine points.

Buying links

Large brands buy links on other sites. It's frowned upon by Google and can lead to penalties. Why is this not acceptable? It's regarded as 'black hat SEO', trying to trick Google algorithms to pretend a site is more important than it actually is.

Nobody knows what Google bases its algorithms on – it's a tightly kept secret. Nevertheless, the more nefarious SEO types keep trying to second-guess it.

The best links are from Wikipedia or the BBC: this means that you have arrived. These are proper kosher sites. Good linking is referred to by SEO types as 'juice', as in 'we want link juice'.

Sometimes, bad sites will link to your site in an attempt to make themselves look legitimate. For instance, when I look at my stats in Blogger, I will get links from bizarre websites that have nothing to do with food. Google can punish the recipient. At one point, the BBC lost its ranking because so many dodgy sites linked to the BBC to gain credibility; fortunately, this was soon rectified. In Hollywood they say 'Don't mess with the mouse' because Disney is so powerful. On the Internet the equivalent is 'Don't aggravate Google'. It can kill a site or a business.

You want honest linking from other sites because you have great content, without having to resort to 'black hat' SEO tactics.

Hyperlinking can fall under copyright law if it gives you an instant snapshot or thumbnail of someone else's content on your page without the reader having to make the effort to go to their site. If this other site is commercial and depends on advertising for revenue, then by hyperlinking you are essentially depriving them of the benefit of their advertising.

Blog roll

This is another useful and legitimate form of links. The more blog rolls your site appears on, the higher in the ranking your blog will go. Today, I've noticed bloggers are less generous with their blog rolls, often hiding them at the bottom of their site or out of the way.

At present, my blog roll is at the side of my blog with a thumbnail picture of the latest post on that blog and a few lines of the first paragraph. My blog roll is primarily to keep me informed about what is happening with other blogs that I am interested in.

Blog roll etiquette: do not ask for inclusion on people's blog rolls. I've had beginner bloggers ask to be on my blog roll. I say no. They need to earn it. Plus, I can choose what I like to be on my own blog roll; it's part of the identity of my blog. I don't appreciate being put under pressure to put somebody's blog on there.

Links within your text

Make sure that you link to your own blog. A blog is an archive. There will be posts that keep yielding stats for years. If you've written a blog post about, say, garlic and later you write a recipe including garlic, make sure that you link to that previous post.

Why link to an outside source if you have a good post on it yourself? This practice is called 'deep linking'.

ETIQUETTE

Copyright

People think once it's on the Internet it's a free for all. It's not. As a content producer, you should know the rules. See the section on recipe copyright in Chapter 3 for more information on that particular aspect of food writing. But generally, no, just because your work is on the Internet, it doesn't mean that anyone gets to use it. Nor does it mean that you can use other people's work. You need:

- permission
- credit
- payment.

For instance, I found that a discount voucher site had used a photograph of mine of a Paris supper club on their site. They did not ask me or credit me. They probably just looked at Google images and took it from there. Why was this wrong? Apart from the obvious – that it's wrong to steal other people's work – you have to consider that I paid to go to Paris, I paid for my camera, I paid for the meal at the supper club. I've also spent years learning about food, making contacts and learning how to photograph well.

I wrote to the company in question and we settled for a fee. They tried to fob me off with a small fee but I insisted on a decent fee. If possible, you want to avoid court. You, as a blogger, probably do not have the resources that a large company has. A letter from a copyright lawyer costs at least £700. Pick your battles.

Libel

Once you are a blogger, you are a publisher. This means that you are responsible for your content and must avoid libel. Forums such as Mumsnet are publishers. Even if you use a pseudonym, your ISP provider could provide the court with your real name and details.

Libel is an intentional attempt to diminish someone's reputation through falsehood. If what you have said is true, it is not libel. So, if you are writing something controversial about a chef, a restaurant, a recipe or a food product, you better make sure that it is true.

At present, the libel laws in England are particularly beneficial for the plaintiff because once accused of libel the defendant has to prove their innocence. This is unlike other areas of the law where you are presumed innocent until proven guilty.

YOUR ARCHIVE

When you have been blogging for a while, you are in the fortunate position of having an archive, a back history of blog posts. Those blog posts keep working on your behalf. For instance, take my blog post, 'How to make your own Marmite'. Boy, does this blog post run and run! Every time there is a Marmite crisis, either because Denmark has banned it as a dangerous substance, or there has been an earthquake in New Zealand at the Marmite factory and supplies are limited, my blog post zooms up the charts in terms of traffic. Marmite lovers are an obsessional bunch, so Marmite has a huge fandom. Frequently, they are unfortunate enough to live in non-Marmite-producing locations and can't get hold of it, so they therefore want to learn how to make it themselves. This post also appeals to geeky types and brewers, as it requires going to a local brewery and getting some of their 'top fermentation'.

Key idea

Great blog posts have a long shelf life. They just keep going.

Most of my other top blog posts are about cake. Cake is eternally appealing. I recently met a publisher who said, confidently, 'Tea is over.' This is rubbish. Tea is never over. When I say 'tea', I mean the afternoon meal with cake. People love cake. I cannot emphasize that enough. Cake is visual, it's easy to photograph prettily, and people are always looking for new recipes or even old recipes reimagined. You can't go wrong with cake.

The food blogger Cook Sister tells me one of her top blog posts was a Brussels sprouts recipe. Every Christmas, people are googling Brussels sprouts recipes and hers is high up in Google rankings.

Unlike cake, Brussels sprouts do not have a sexy reputation and, even though Brussels sprouts are frequently eaten, they are not often blogged about. Blogging about a humdrum vegetable, with a great recipe, will reap dividends.

 Key idea

'Evergreen content' refers to a blog post that has a very long shelf life. In terms of food blogging, it's not niche, it usually has standard ingredients and is a recipe that will continue to get hits for a long time.

BLOG DESIGN: HOW TO MAKE YOUR BLOG LOOK GORGEOUS

Blogs are visually driven: you may just want to write but if you want to get readers, you need the visual – either drawings or photos – plus good design. Reading on the backlit screen is difficult and pictures break up the text. As they say, a picture tells a thousand words.

Here are a few design tips:

- Work out a colour palette that suits you and that is consistent throughout your brand. Use only two or three colours.
- Text must be dark against a pale background. When you first start blogging you will be tempted to experiment with every colour and every template. 'Ooh, look at the pretty colours!', you will think. But think of readability. People can read it so much more easily if it's black text on white. In the old days people who wrote using 'green link' were thought of as lunatics; nowadays, in the Internet age, the same dictum could be applied to people who use any brightly coloured font. Don't do it: it will make you look like a loony.
- Use the same font/fonts throughout your brand. Use only two or three throughout your blog. There are sites where you can get free fonts such as fontsquirrel.com. There are two main types of font: serif and sans serif. Serifs are the ends of letters, the little 'hooks'. Sans serif is more modern; serif is more classic. There are some studies that say serif fonts are easier to read for the main body of the text but on a computer screen

sans serif is preferable. Script fonts, in particular, are hard to read. So, when choosing a font, consider readability and style. Don't use the font Comic Sans under any circumstances, unless it's as a joke.

- Check your blog is looking fresh. Make sure it's looking '2015' (or whatever year you happen to be reading this). Regularly update the look of your blog. Think of it like make-up: you don't want 1950s winged eyeliner if it dates you. Same with blog design.

- Use of white space is very important. Embrace it. Don't clutter your blog.

- Get a logo designed. You can get this done very cheaply starting from £20. Just do a web search for logo design.

- Make your online presence consistent with your blog so that you have a visually recognizable brand. Pinterest, Instagram, Twitter, Facebook – keep them to one style across every platform.

- Make sure that your blog is easy to read on different formats and test it out on iPads/tablets and iPhones/Android phones. It has to be responsive on mobile and should display in the same way.

- Your header is the first impression of your blog. It must be clean and crisp, using a good photo or illustration. Think about an effective strapline – the words that describe your blog in simple terms.

- In design terms, people read from left to right in Western cultures. So usually the sidebar is on the right-hand side. You want to lead with your content, which is the main 'body' of your blog.

- Text and photos should all align. You will notice that many blogs have all of their photos landscape or horizontal. In Blogger, without a specially designed template, this is one of the few ways to make sure that all of your photos and text are aligned. Left aligned is how we read.

- How people navigate their way about your blog is something worth thinking about. Will it be a pick and mix of delightful discoveries? Or will it be linear/chronological?

- The content of your blog is your USP (unique selling point).

- In terms of readability, don't overwhelm people. Break it up with photographs. A blog post should be over 250 words but not too long, so probably under 750 words. People simply can't read much on screen. People remember only 7 per cent of any book they read, or so I've heard. Imagine how much they take in from your blog. That's why bloggers like a) lists and b) bullet points.
- Sidebars can be a wonderful distraction, but don't overdo them. Widgets clutter blogs, so stick to a few. Try to have no more than five down the side. Obvious ones to include (though some of these can be put as tabs or pages on your site) are:
  - A **picture of you** and your email address (probably near the top).
  - A **sign-up box** to be a subscriber to your blog and/or your newsletter. You need a sign-up form because this is how you will build your data base. It is very important that this is in a prominent place. You can also put it in your header/footer and under each post.
  - **About you.** This can also be a tab. Below the basic information, you should have something about the mission of your blog. You could also have a media pack or a policy statement such as 'I don't do sponsored posts nor do I accept gifts from PRs' or 'If you wish me to review something on my blog, I'm happy to accept your invitation but on the understanding that I will be truthful' or ' If you would like me to write recipes or host competitions please write to me at this address for my list of fees.'
  - **The search facility** on your blog. Make sure that it is easy to find and that it is high up in your sidebar.
  - **Your most popular blog posts** or more useful blog posts. Or perhaps a downloadable PDF of your ebook.
  - **Links to your social media** such as Twitter, Facebook and Pinterest.
  - **Testimonials.** Add some quotes from fans, from celebrities, even from haters. Use tweets as testimonials. I did have a whole section devoted to quotes about my work. I also put up positive quotes from press reviews about my supper club and

my book. Along with quotes, mention your awards. People love awards. I would avoid all those made-up awards from other bloggers with sparkly bears and stuff – unless you are into that kind of 'cute' and your audience is into it, too.

- **Blog roll.** It's a shame that so many bloggers are extremely ungenerous about other blogs nowadays. I'm a great fan of the blog roll. Put it somewhere fairly obvious. Share the love. It's what blogging is supposed to be about.

- **Adverts** or affiliate links.

> ## Key idea
>
> Google analytics can tell you which of your sidebar features are attracting visitors.

- The footer is not a dumping ground. It can be used as a sidebar but don't overload it. You can put contact details there and copyright information.
- Learn about the fold: as in a magazine or newspaper, is something above or below the fold? Above the fold is where all your important information, your big stories should be. This is the portion of your site that is visible without having to scroll. The fold is important when it comes to search engines, too. Most people use the sites on page one, above the fold.
- When you are happy with design make sure that you spread that design over all of your work: your email signature, your blog business cards, your photos.
- Make sure everything works on your site – that there are no error pages. Double-check spelling.

> ## Key idea
>
> Less is more. Do be careful of GIFs and flashing images. Music is a total no-no. These are all distractions from your content.

Key idea

Get some genuine critiques. Ask friends to be your blog buddy.
You need constructive feedback and this is a great way of making
improvements.

TRAFFIC

Page rank is a way of measuring the importance of websites. It used
to be vital but nowadays it is less so.

BLOG RANKINGS

There are various sites purporting to show the number-one food
blog. Trouble is, most of these are based on page hits, which is not
necessarily a good indicator of how influential or how popular the
blog is. Many of the so-called top blogs rely on competitions and
free giveaways to garner hundreds of comments.

Key idea

Encourage engagement. Blogging is a two-way process, so do
involve your readers. Writing a question at the end of a blog post
is another way of reaching out.

SUBSCRIBERS AND NEWSLETTERS

How to make subscribing easy? Do a weekly newsletter, ask people
to sign up, right at the top of your site. You have a captive audience
with readers. Preview changes; share them. Ask readers what they
think. Do so during the process rather than at the end.

I would recommend signing up with Mailchimp to send a monthly
newsletter. Mailchimp used to be very difficult to use but is now
very easy with a drag-and-drop feature. You can drop in your blog
header and photos from your blog posts. Newsletters are a real
driver of traffic.

How to work with PRs

I get sent free products all the time and once you are established as a food blogger, you will too. That's fun. I always make clear that I probably won't write about them. Sometimes I do write about them. Sometimes, if I feel the product is worthy of mention but I haven't got time to write a blog post, I'll tweet or Instagram the product, mentioning it, just as a courtesy. What PRs want is to be able to go back to their client and say 'Look, so and so of this blog mentioned your product, so yes, I am doing my job.' In fact, PRs love bloggers because it gives them fast results. Bloggers tend to be more grateful for freebies, work more quickly, have shorter lead-in times, have more space to write and photograph the product. They also have a specialist audience. In addition, as I mentioned earlier, research has shown that people are more influenced by 'peers' than celebrities or journalists. A blogger is a 'peer', a friend that you can talk to and interact with in the comments.

I remember getting my first freebie, a polystyrene cool box of smoothies. I was so thrilled. I felt like a Hollywood star and strutted around my kitchen punching the air in triumph. (And I wasn't even that keen on the smoothies.) Now this happens so often that I am more blasé. It's still nice, though.

There is a downside, however, which is that I get relentless emails from PRs asking 'Did you like it?', 'Have you written about it?', 'Can you send me the link?'. There is no such thing as a free lunch in food blogging. They expect quid pro quo. Sometimes, if you really don't like the product, you just say so: 'I'm afraid I wasn't too keen on your instant stir-in sauce/electric fryer/meal in a restaurant.' The last thing PRs want is a bad review, so they will leave you alone after that. But don't abuse the fact you get freebies. It is one of the perks. PRs have a job to do; they are human too (believe it or not).

Sally Whittle of Foodies100 agrees with me that there has been a PR takeover of blogging: 'Five years ago, brands weren't interested at all in social media.' I remember going to a Jamie Oliver event at Debenhams in 2009. He had several PR companies there: one for him, one for Debenhams, one for the cookware range. One PR agency, who saw me tweeting about the event, approached me. They were clueless about social media; they didn't even know how to get on Twitter and asked whether they could buy me lunch to find out. Things have changed so much: now most PRs have a digital division.

Today, brands are more forward-thinking in aiming for creative content – for instance recipe development work with food bloggers. As digital PR budgets get bigger, campaigns will become more interesting. They won't just be asking bloggers to do sponsored posts; they will create campaigns in conjunction with bloggers. Each department of a marketing and PR firm will have different budget pots and social media used to have the smallest budget of any campaign. That has changed. Marketing, PR and their clients are allocating more money to this aspect of their promotional campaigns and the average contract value is much higher.

If you work consistently on the quality of your blog, it's worth PR agencies working with you over the long term. This is called **long-tail PR**. Your reputation enhances the reputation of their brand. This is a slow-burner but a highly influential technique. Blogging is virtual word of mouth: they spread the message peer to peer. Long tail also caters to niche tastes, which bloggers cater for. So if you have a blog that only writes about burgers, on a quest for the perfect burger experience, then the smart brand gets you on board to write about its ketchup/buns/pickle. Most marketing and advertising works on a popularity principle: if a brand has mass sales, then there is the budget to advertise. Blogging/vlogging/social media are the reverse: they enable advertising of things that don't have mass appeal. Although things are moving rapidly: vlogging, most famously in the form of beauty vlogger Zoella, is being sought after by the big brands, too.

Mirror brand strategy is marketing speak for a brand that wants to reflect its demographic. This is where bloggers come in. A blogger, not being a celebrity or a paid journalist, reflects their audience. If they like it, if they can be bothered to write about it, then people will buy it.

 Key idea

Keep it real: value lies with personal perspective. Savvy readers can spot the difference between editorial and advertorial. But the future lies in partnerships between brands and bloggers.

Write

Write three blog posts, each using a different approach:

1 **A tutorial, a 'how to':** for example, how to make lasagne, or how to make a Victoria sponge.

2 **A top ten list:** it could be the top ten coffee shops in your area, or top five fruit and veg shops.

3 **A review:** review a series of food products. These need not be expensive – it could be a range of ice creams or crisps. Take a picture of each and work out a system for scoring them, which could be based on flavour, packaging, nutrition and so on.

Interviews

SALLY WHITTLE, FOUNDER OF FOODIES100.COM

A former technology journalist, Sally was writing for broadsheets in the UK and the United States. Her personal blog, after she had a baby, had become, in her words, 'a weird hybrid of parenting and technology'. As a result of dipping into this world, Sally realized that there was a very strong community of parent blogs and started Tots100.

What inspired you to start Foodies100?

In journalism, there are media databases but no equivalent for social media, which is not ranked in the same way. I started in a small way, from home, doing it all by hand on Excel sheets, in 2009. Knowing lots of geeks was really helpful. Eventually, I found a publisher who would develop and automate the site.

After the success of Tots100, I realized that brands wanted to talk to food bloggers, who had a very active community, probably the closest and most interesting community after parent bloggers. Foodies100 is only five years old.

How did you find food bloggers after working with 'mummy bloggers'?

It was much harder to break into the food blogging community than the parent bloggers. Many food bloggers were a little bit suspicious of what we were doing. I must admit I can't cook myself. I once made biscuits but they looked like cat sick.

Tell me how you do the Foodies100.com rankings? They tend to come up with very different results from other food blogger charts.

It was important to have different metrics. We were trying to avoid people 'gaming it'. All the different metrics sanity-check one other. The metrics we use now aren't the same metrics that we used five years ago. We now have 4,000 food blogs.

On Wikio, for instance, now called Ebuzzing, it's all about backlinks and it can be a circle of bloggers referring to one other in posts. [Author note: I can confirm this. I know that the top four on Wikio were deliberately gaming the system, linking to one other in their blogposts. Consequently, they remained at the top of the rankings for about a year. How do I know this? They told me.]

To do well in the Foodies100 rankings, for a start the blog has to be popular and has to have plenty of traffic. Foodies 100 is the only one that tracks traffic.

Other considerations for the Foodies100 chart are:

- **engagement:** partly comments, but mostly shares, mentions on Twitter, Facebook and backlinks
- **recency of links:** if you haven't blogged for six months, you drop down, which allows newer bloggers to rise up.

Twenty-five per cent of the ranking is based on Pinterest. You can get a lot of traffic from Pinterest and being popular on Pinterest will help your rank. However the system is never perfect. We cannot measure quality.

What do you think about bloggers who carry sponsored posts and do traffic-boosting giveaways?

I think: more power to them! After all, blogging is a new industry that is very female-centric. It enables women to stay at home, look after their children, and work around their hours. Blogging is very empowering for women. Although for some it is just a hobby.

What general direction will blogging take in the future, in your opinion?

I think blogging will become more commercial.

HELEN GRAVES OF FOOD STORIES BLOG

> *Helen Graves was joint winner of the 2013 Young British Foodies online food writing awards.*

Tell me about your blog and what led you to it.

I'm 34 years old. I trained as a psychologist. At university, I started to cook. By 2004, I was reading other blogs. It was a new way to write about food. I wanted to do something creative besides my degree.

I've been blogging for seven years, since July 2007. In 2007 I started on Blogger. My header had a really bad font! I grew up online. I didn't know what I was doing. I got it redesigned in 2010. I spent around £300 to make my blog look more professional. In 2012 I thought: 'There is no point', because I could never do it. It was a confidence issue. I've had a shaky patch recently thinking, 'What is my blog about?' Now I'm on a self-hosted WordPress blog. At the moment, I've decided to reinvest in my blog and spend around £1,000 to redesign it. This is the second redesign. [Author note: This is proof that you constantly have to update and improve your blog repeatedly. You can't stand still.] It started out as a hobby but now I want to be a professional food blogger. And I'm leaving my full-time job in September.

Now I want to stick to recipes and travel. I was serious about sandwiches – my other blog was the London Review of Sandwiches [which led to a book], which I started in 2012. But blogging needs so much hard work to keep it going.

Any advice on how to write a blog?

- Try to avoid clichés.
- Sit on things. Go away; come back to it. Don't rush anything. Sit back.
- Learn to edit properly. Sentence by sentence. Ask yourself: is that adding anything? Am I saying the same thing again and again?
- Stay true to your own style.
- Be in the mood. Write your blog when you are in the mood. Books are different. You've got to be disciplined. You can't just write when you feel like it.

- Just write until you are finished. Sometimes I write just a paragraph. My travel posts are long, though.
- Try to create value for a reader. Work out what your thing is and run with it.
- If you are funny or know about a certain subject, use that.
- It's got to be entertaining and informative, and look amazing.
- You've got to have half-decent pictures. Photos break up the text. If the photos are awful, it looks as though you don't care.
- The competition is stiff. American blogs are really professional. But they are often sentimental and twee.

How often do you blog?

At the moment, once every two weeks. But, other times, a few times a week, three times a week.

What food writers do you admire?

Diana Henry, Sally Butcher, Diana Kennedy. I love an in-depth cookbook. I'm nerdy.

Now you've got several book deals, will you continue to blog?

I would never want to give up my blog, ever. I love that, the freedom of it.

I made a mistake on my books. I shouldn't have accepted the second book deal. Nor the third one. I don't want to do any more gift books.

It's hard to make money when you don't have a full-time job to make up your income.

I supplement my income with sales of the jerk marinade. I got some paid food writing with *Sainsbury's Magazine*. I'm doing a master class for *The Guardian*: 'Turn your blog into a book'.

Ultimately, I'd like to write about travel and food.

FUSS-FREE HELEN (HELEN BEST-SHAW)

Helen Best-Shaw has been blogging since 2007. She's on a self-hosted WordPress blog. She figured out how to do much of the technical stuff required to set it up herself, but she hired a designer and a developer to give her current site a professional look. Helen advises hiring both.

You used to work in the City – why did you change to working with food?

Although I worked in the City I always cooked. At weekends, I would batch cook for the week. Maybe I bought a sandwich once a week. Frozen soup is particularly good: you take frozen soup to work, it doesn't leak because it's solid, then I would heat it up in the work microwave.

I was quite active on forums talking about food. I would discuss, for instance, that there was a lovely market next to me but people were shopping for £1 ready-meals in discount supermarkets.

How did you learn to cook?

My mother taught me to cook from scratch. Nowadays at school, kids are more likely to learn how to design the packaging in food technology courses than learn how to cook a meal. Nowadays it's actually cheaper to buy a ready-meal than cook from scratch.

Tell me what it was like to be a food blogger at the beginning?

When I started blogging, it was all recipe writing. There was no Twitter, no Facebook pages, no PR companies. Now it seems that the world and his wife has a food blog. In 2007 not every house even had a computer. I had to go to an Internet cafe to get on the Internet. I really started blogging once I got a digital camera and a laptop. Now you can blog with a phone, set up a blog in ten minutes. There were no iPhones. This has transformed the landscape.

What has been the effect of PRs and marketing on blogging?

My first blogging event was with Tilda rice in July 2010. It is possible to work with brands but you must negotiate when, how much, and what you are doing for a brand. Writing an original recipe gives readers value. For example, I recently wrote a coconut roti recipe for a Mauritian hotel. But I've also visited Mauritius in the past, so I could use some of that experience to write up an interesting, although sponsored, blog post.

I use agencies to get work and I'm making a fairly good living at it. Blogging is the best thing I've ever done. I spent today cooking with Monica Galetti and Michel Roux Jr. Money couldn't buy this. I'm really enjoying this but it's taken a long time to get to my position. When you are invited to events, your entertainment is paid for.

I earned less than minimum wage for the first few years and I've been blogging full time for the last four years.

What advice do you have for new bloggers?

If you start a blog for fun, don't expect to get things straight away. The people who have been longer established are fortunate, they have an archive.

The Internet is ultimately search-driven. Having a profile on the Internet is very much how Google sees you. We are a few years behind the USA, which is a bigger country and the Internet/blogging is more advanced. But you will always have to diversify, stay on your toes, keep up to date. Pay-per-view ads are not a good revenue stream anymore. It was good in 2010–11.

You have to promote yourself via social media. You have to write beautifully and honestly. I've turned down brands and money because they clash with my ethics or with other brands I promote. You can't one day write about compassion in world farming then take a hamper from, say, Red Tractor. Understand your value. Don't sell yourself short. Remember that nobody is sending you stuff out of the goodness of their heart. It's a transaction. My main advice is, when it comes to working with brands, if it doesn't feel right, don't do it.

CHRIS POPLE OF CHEESE AND BISCUITS

> Chris Pople is probably the UK's top restaurant blogger, a close friend of Fay Maschler's and a stalwart of the Evening Standard's 1,000 Most Influential Londoners list. He writes well and has recently even learned to photograph food, too.

How do you manage the ethics of getting a free meal?

If you get a free meal, you must declare that it is free. You must declare on your blog: 'I was a guest of …' The issue of free meals is a difficult one. Obviously, as a blogger, you don't get paid – therefore why not accept the odd free meal? Blogging is supposed to be fun and enjoyable and this is one of the benefits. But you must be honest otherwise your readers will no longer trust you to be impartial. At the same time, you have to balance the fact that if you want free meals, don't slag everything off or you won't be offered anything else.

How many times do you visit a restaurant before reviewing it?

In the UK, a food writer usually visits a restaurant once, so you aren't going to be able to try everything on the menu. [Author note: in the States, at least in pre-recession times, professional restaurant reviewers such as Ruth Reichl would visit a restaurant several times before writing a review.] So, the way around this is to look at other people's food. What are they eating? Does it look good?

Also, if you think you are being treated better than others in the restaurant, either because you are a known food writer, or because you are photographing the food, look at how others are treated.

Do you book in your own name or anonymously?

Do you want to enjoy yourself or be a martyr to the cause? If you are an unpaid blogger, well yes, you want a few perks. For instance, I visited the The Chiltern Firehouse where everyone from David Cameron to Lindsay Lohan was visiting, but chef Nuno Mendes came out and said hello to me, ignoring all the celebrities. Moments like that make it all worthwhile.

Can you tell me about your approach to writing?

No one ever told me how to do it. My approach is to think of a story about the restaurant, an angle. I try to come up with something topical, not just about the restaurant, and put the review in a context. People need a story, so you take a general subject such as gastropubs or French restaurants in London and, using a few pertinent introductory comments on the state of play in this area, then go on to specifics about the restaurant you have visited. For instance, there may have been a story in the news about bad food hygiene in a Chinese restaurant and you are visiting a Chinese restaurant. Then you would talk about the food hygiene in the review.

I tend to write about a meal sequentially, in chronological, course order. The great advantage about blogs is that the writer has space: there is no word count and, of course, a photo of each course is possible. Writing about a restaurant in a newspaper or magazine, for instance, you will have restricted space and maybe only one or two photos: generally a photograph of an empty restaurant and perhaps one dish.

Another approach is to pick out the highlights of the meal, especially when you are having, say, a 20-course tasting menu. (There was a blogger, Food Snob, who used to lovingly detail every aspect, each ingredient and how it was cooked, of every course. It made for tedious reading but chefs simply loved his blog. It was total food geekery in the trainspotting style.)

How do you choose your restaurant?

Nowadays, because I'm well known, it's often via freebies. And the freebies I accept tend to be posh, expensive restaurants, stuff I couldn't normally afford. A cheap restaurant I can afford.

Do you ever give a negative review of the posh freebies?

Yes... One restaurant I was invited to cost £400 a head. I could never afford that. It was all very impressive but the food was very average. It was crowd-pleasing international business traveller food. (In fact, most expensive, Michelin-star-type restaurants serve this kind of food.)

What is the difference between a restaurant reviewing blog and a recipe blog?

The creativity with a restaurant review blog starts with the writing. With a cookery blog, the creativity is all in the cooking, while the write-up is a breeze.

How many times a week do you publish?

I do about five or six reviews a month. Never publish at the weekend. Publish during the week when people are at work and want a chance to skive off. Of course, if the content is good, you can publish anytime.

Do you still enjoy it?

I enjoy it when it's over, when you get feedback. It's a bit like going to the gym, a tremendous effort which you have to make yourself do, but you feel good afterwards. I don't go to everything I'm invited to.

What kind of restaurants do people want to read about?

New places and expensive places get huge hits.

How do you afford it?

Most restaurant bloggers are posh, with fantastic disposable incomes. They tend to be geeky males, trainspotter types. Plus you have to be a certain type: quite harsh.

Do you reply to comments below the line?

I don't reply to comments, unless the commenter is asking a genuine question. [Author note: I would recommend, in the early days, that you, as a new blogger, do comment on lots of other blogs. You will be noticed!]

What about the future of restaurant blogging?

I don't see any new ones coming through. Established food bloggers are moving on to other things – writing books, setting up restaurants, food consultancy, PR.

Do you want to become a paid restaurant reviewer for a paper?

I've given up on my early ambition of being paid as a restaurant reviewer, getting a column. There are no new restaurant columns; in fact, restaurant reviewers are being laid off. The entire restaurant review pages of *Metro* newspaper, for instance, were cancelled and everyone sacked.

In terms of paid work, I write online for Groupon, doing 'five best restaurant' type pieces, for which I'm paid £100 a post. Which is not that much per piece but it can build up to a nice monthly sum if several of my pitches are successful. I also write for Joe Warwick who does an annual book, *Where Chefs Eat*.

Do you have influence? Do your reviews make a difference?

Yes. Chefs and restaurant owners have told me they get loads of extra bookings if I do a good review of their restaurant. For instance, the Indian restaurant Trishna, they got 100 reservations on the back of my article. That's well worth the price of a free meal.

And my review of Peckham Bazaar got them more bookings from my review than Fay Maschler's review in the *Evening Standard*.

Could that be because your readership is different from Fay's?

Yes, I think my readership has a lower income and is more foodie than Fay's. Fay is just one section of a newspaper whereas people who read my blog have specifically chosen to read it. That's why the page hit thing is bogus. I get 30,000 page views per month but each of them means something.

Any more tips?

- Socialize with other restaurant bloggers, go to blogging events, especially in the early days.

- Love what you do and only write about what you love. You can only write well that way.
- Protect your brand. No amount of money is worth ruining your reputation. Even if I was offered 10,000 to write a positive review about a terrible chain restaurant, that wouldn't compensate for the damage it would do to my blog, which I've spent ten years building up.

 ## Chris Pople

'If you are not very good, blog often. While you are finding your voice, your style and your niche, blog as often as you can to build up a following.'

 ## Write exercise

Write a restaurant review blog, including pictures if you can. Try to imagine useful things that a reader/potential customer will want to know, such as:
- the best place to sit
- what to order
- the best dishes
- whether it is value for money
- whether the service is good.

 ## Helen of Fuss Free

'The future is extremely rosy for bloggers.'

Next step

In the next chapter we'll look at how you can get people to read your work and build a profile using social media.

7

Promoting your food writing using social media

This chapter will give you some advice on using social media to boost your profile as a food writer. If you are already writing for a newspaper or magazine, this isn't as necessary as if you are a blogger, where you have to bang your drum for a while to get noticed. What you are doing is using social networks to promote your brand.

At the end of this chapter you will also get some advice on how to make sure that your online presence is known.

Branding

It might sound very contrived but you need to create a brand, in other words turn yourself into a online personality with a USP (unique selling point). Some of you may be more comfortable with that than others. But actually all you are doing is framing, for public consumption, what you are about, who you are and what you write about. It's nothing more sinister than that. Your personality may be very quiet, very shy. That's OK, too. There's no point pretending to be anybody else. The thing about social media is that you will soon be found out if you are not being yourself. Transparency and authenticity are the keywords. This is why it's difficult for the large brands on Twitter and Facebook: who is the personality they are trying to promote? The best Twitter feeds and Facebook pages are always written by people who care about their business.

However, at the same time branding always involves a degree of self-editing, showing the best side of yourself, just as you would at a party or any social occasion. You wouldn't go in scruffy clothes, so when creating a brand, you have to think hard about how you want to present yourself. That isn't to say you will present a fake self, just an enhanced self.

Sometimes this can occur by accident, and in some ways that's the best method. My 'brand' was completely organic, that is, it evolved naturally rather than by design. I named myself MsMarmitelover on my blog and Twitter because I was afraid of being arrested. When I started my supper club, a restaurant in my living room, The Underground Restaurant, I wasn't sure how legal it was. I didn't want anyone to know my real name, what I looked like or where I lived. The more secret I was, the more excited people became. At first my only 'avatar' (the small photo or image you have on, say, Twitter or on your Facebook profile) was my eye or my lips. So for two years nobody knew who I was. Once my book was published, in 2011, my real name and what I looked like were revealed.

Once you have a brand, you need to disseminate it via social media. Your brand can and will change over time. This will occur ordinarily and in the usual way, but you should also, on a yearly basis, update your avatar/photo and biography to reflect what you are doing.

To give an idea of the importance of social media: in 2010, it was estimated that 87 per cent of bloggers used Facebook while 78 per cent of bloggers used Twitter. A large proportion of these use both Twitter and Facebook to promote their blogs. Now, I suspect, it's 100 per cent.

There are so many social media platforms but I will deal with the main players as of 2015. However, be aware that social networking platforms come in and out of fashion – it's a fickle business. Remember MySpace? MySpace, while remaining important for musicians, is an empty space. Poor old Tom has no friends anymore.

Here we will look at Twitter, Facebook, Instagram, Pinterest and Google Plus in detail and then at a few others in brief. It's probably worth registering your name/brand on each of these just to reserve your place and prevent others using it. But I'd advise that you choose two to three platforms and do them well. Don't spread yourself too thinly.

Never forget that the writing – the content of your work – is the main thing. If you spend your whole time on social media, when do you get to write?

Twitter

Twitter is particularly good for time sensitive social media – it's instant news boiled down to 140 characters. It often gets the news before the *News*. Remember the Bin Laden raid? A local guy living nearby tweeted about mysterious helicopters and noise around the then-unknown Bin Laden compound in the middle of the night. We were hearing about the raid in real time from a citizen journalist. Twitter has also contributed to activism, being an anonymous way to get the message out, particularly during the Arab Spring. But Twitter has become a problem: libellous and/or threatening tweets have been made about public figures or women espousing feminist views.

Twitter is like gossiping over the garden fence with the neighbours about what is going on, but on a global level. The media loves Twitter, which is why so many news reports now contain embedded Twitter quotes. Twitter is extremely useful, even for well-known professional journalists. Being a writer is isolating, and it's a way of socializing online. It's also great for asking the Twitter 'hive mind' for advice, contacts and ideas.

Twitter is now ten years old, so it's quite a mature platform. It used to be more about affinity, *who* you liked. While fewer people use Twitter than Facebook, they use Twitter more frequently. Tweeting is now very competitive: people want to be the best, the one with the most followers. This is understandable: lots of followers means influence. It impresses PRs and other brands. For instance, the tourist board of Japan had the budget to bring a UK food writer to Japan for an all-expenses-paid trip. They were going to send Marina O'Loughlin, a well-respected food and travel writer who works for *The Guardian* and *Olive* magazine. But they bumped her off the trip in order to send blogger Niamh Shields of *Eat Like a Girl*. Why? Because Niamh has more followers on Twitter. The fact that Marina is an award-winning national newspaper writer made no odds to them; they were impressed by Twitter followers instead. This sounds crazy especially in a world where people can buy fake followers (I'm not saying Niamh does this – she has slowly and organically built up a Twitter following the hard way). But it's estimated that 71 per cent of Lady Gaga's 35 million followers are fake. What is important is the quality of followers, not just the numbers; you want genuine interactive long-term followers and well-respected peers from your field. Plus a sprinkling of star dust if you can get the odd celebrity to follow you.

Some tweeters are so good, so humorous and so witty within the strict 140-character limit that they get paid to tweet for other people. For instance, Greg Stekelman also known as @Themanwhofell had a droll online personality which was very funny. He was making people laugh all day for free. Eventually, he gave up his Twitter profile and started tweeting professionally for Betfair.

Many of the stars of Twitter have ghosted tweets but in general Twitter has been a godsend for celebrities. It means they can get their message out without the press acting as middleman. Some celebrities have also made mistakes, tweeting unacceptable opinions that lead to ruin. It's a fine line between authenticity and presenting your best face to the public.

A BEGINNER'S GUIDE TO TWITTER (WITH ADDITIONAL INFORMATION FROM EVA KEOGAN OF HOMEOFSOCIAL.COM)

At first Twitter can feel strange and not make sense. You have to gather a few followers before you feel like you are part of the conversation. How do you do that?

Following and being followed

You will be asked, when you sign up to Twitter, to choose categories of interest such as news, sport, entertainment. Then they will ask you to follow 40 accounts, then another 20. The accounts they suggest will tend to be 'verified' celebrities (that means having a blue tick to prove that you are famous) so, unless you want to follow the casts of various reality-TV shows, look for good people to follow.

They will oblige you to add everyone from your address book. (If you really don't want to do this, start a new 'clean' email account.)

Follow other writers, peer groups, influencers in the area you are interested in. In the world of food that will be food writers, restaurant reviewers, bloggers, chefs, suppliers.

RT (retweet) and 'favourite' their tweets. They will be able to see that and will appreciate it. Build up that relationship. There is an art to that – it takes time.

I'm followed by Giles Coren. How? I met him at an event and asked him. I said: 'Can you follow me on Twitter?' He balked slightly and said, 'The way to do well on Twitter is get someone famous to follow you.' I said I knew and that's why I was asking him. 'How many times a day do you tweet?' he asked. 'I don't want to be overwhelmed.' 'About ten times a day?' I ventured. I didn't think he'd do it but the next day sure enough he followed me. He only follows 422 people and I'm one of them. Hooray!

Sometimes it's just luck that gets you followers. At the beginning, in 2009, John Cleese noticed my account on Twitter and tweeted about Marmite and me. Overnight I got 800 followers – it was quite exhilarating. This was so unusual that it was mentioned in the national press. Now, people are always asking celebrities to recommend them to be followed.

On Twitter if you have over 500 followers that is a good amount – something that PRs will take seriously. At the same time, aim to follow 500 accounts.

Follower to followed differential

Personally, I think this is playground politics for adults – a digital 'mean girls'. You are considered cool if you don't follow many people back. I think that's horrible. But apparently that's how Twitter wants it to work: you follow only who interests you or is useful to you and you attempt to amass as many followers as you can. If you follow this technique and are not generous about following back, then at least make sure that you are not just 'broadcasting', that you are interacting, even if you don't follow.

Tweeting

You should tweet between 8 and 22 times a day to achieve a branded profile.

The best times to tweet are before an event, at an event, after an event. If you speak at that event, this is a great time to get other followers. You will get advocacy and thanks. Tweet from the back room. Create or use the hashtag for the event.

Another way to get followers is to tweet around TV shows, like cookery shows. Tweet people you admire. If it's spot on, they may respond.

When people follow you, with every ten new followers, thank them.

Thank people for an RT.

Do Follow Friday – #FF – which is when you recommend other people to follow, yup, on a Friday. Don't just put the names, say why people should follow them.

Hashtags

These are a way of finding communities and events on Twitter. Any event manager worth their salt will set up a short, easy hashtag. This means that, if it's a large event, you can find others in the same room, attending the same event, by their Twitter hashtags.

Do relevant hashtags: #Meatfreemonday #Traveltuesday. Also #bizhour #Amwriting which runs 24/7. Writers ask for advice.

You can also set up your own hashtag to create a blogger 'carnival'.

Ask for RTs for special causes, charities or issues (but don't abuse this).

When to tweet

The best time is after 9 p.m., when people have arrived home and had a glass of wine. You'll get the conversations, especially about TV programmes. Another good time is after 10 a.m. and before 4 p.m., midweek, when people are bored at work. There are also hours which are region specific: if you want to attract an American audience, tweet during the night.

Smart brands will have their 'community managers', as they are euphemistically called (it sounds as though they are performing a public service, doesn't it?), working out of hours.

Using the Twitter hive mind

You can crowdsource recipes, for instance. I've done this. Once I was stuck for a menu theme and recipes for a supper club. I put the word out asking what I should cook that Saturday. Radio presenter and writer Hardeep Singh Kohli responded with a recipe idea. I then asked him whether he wanted to help me cook and he agreed! I once asked for help when a fish supplier delivered me 40 sea bass that hadn't (despite my instructions) been cleaned and gutted. Within moments a chef on Twitter said, 'I'll come over and help you gut them.' This chef – @garyrobinson – turned out to be Prince Charles's former chef, boy-band good-looking and with a discreet supply of gossip. He'd literally cooked for everyone from the Dalai Lama to Madonna and Michael Jackson.

Gary stood there looking immaculate, having arrived in his flash sports car, and cleaned 40 fish for me in a couple of hours. It would have taken me all day. He then guest-cheffed when I did a royal-wedding dinner. Brilliant. All from a tweet!

Some dos...

Tweet pictures – photos uploaded directly to Twitter.

Shout a bit. Be good company. Be lively, chatty, funny.

Tweet your blog posts. You can set up an automatic feed on Twitter widgets, for instance Twitterfeed.

Tweet while cooking.

Tweet while travelling.

Tweet in restaurants.

...and don'ts

Some people have a tin ear for the music of Twitter. They just don't get it. For instance, it's not cool to hijack somebody's following or to hijack a hashtag.

Some tips

> *Eva Keogan advises companies how to manage their social media, across all platforms. She teaches workshops and gives lectures on the subject. Here are her tips for building up a Twitter following:*

Here are Eva Keogan's social-media musts... all relevant to Twitter:

- Try to use the same name across all of your social media.
- Make sure that your profile picture is memorable and use the same avatar/photo across all of your social media.
- The 'header' on your Twitter profile should be interesting and colourful, representing your blog or your brand. On Twitter there is also a background: use this as an advertising hoarding. It could be comments, quotes, or your email. It could be your book cover or your ebook. It should be an insight into your world. Make sure that you use that previous digital real estate effectively.
- Avoid mismatched cover pages on Facebook/LinkedIn/YouTube/Google Plus: again, make sure that all of your social media matches up, so readers will know at a glance that it's you.

- Make sure that your biography (bio) is complete and without mistakes. You have just 160 characters on your Twitter bio, so use them effectively. Explain who you are. You can also give people a flavour of the tweets they will get – for example: 'Follow me for tweets about...' Do make sure that you spellcheck the words. This is your online mini CV.
- Use keywords such as food, foodie, writer, blogger, author, published writer, chef, where you are based, the link to your blog. Add your location – this is very important.
- Make sure that you include your blog URL on your bio (obviously!). But also make a virtuous circle of social media by linking all of your differing social media feeds. For instance, if I Instagram something, it will go on to my public Facebook page, which will then feed on to my Twitter stream. See! One photo, three places that it will go.

Snapshot exercise

Set up your Twitter account now. Choose your name, upload a picture, write your biography, set a background and a banner header. Set your location. Link it to your blog or site. Send your first tweet...

Facebook

Facebook is the world's most popular social networking site. One-sixth of the world's population is on Facebook. You can't ignore it, so use it. The demographics of Facebook have changed: younger users are decreasing, probably because older users are using it. Facebook is worldwide, whereas Twitter is particularly popular in the UK and the United States but less so in Europe.

Start a Facebook page for your blog/website/business that is different from your personal Facebook. This is a way to direct readers to your blog via NetworkedBlogs (networkedblogs.com).

Keep your branding consistent. For instance, I recently changed my Facebook page from The Underground Restaurant, which is the name of my supper club, to MsMarmiteLover, which has, over time, become my best-known 'name'. Try to get it right first time, but you can apply to Facebook, as I did, to change the name of the page. If your blog's name is AliceJones, make sure that you have a Twitter @AliceJones, an official Facebook page Alice Jones (as opposed to your personal one) and get @AliceJones on Instagram. If your name is quite a common one, like Alice Jones, it might be a good idea to choose another name or title. If you are a baker, and your blog is mainly about cakes and baking, perhaps choose @Alicebakes, a Facebook page Alice Bakes and so on.

Some tips

- Use photos on your updates/posts: they generate more engagement than just a written phrase.
- Keep your Facebook posts short, fewer than 250 characters.
- Thursday and Friday are the most popular days of the week for responses.
- Ask questions. Posts that end with a question mark are twice as popular.

Snapshot exercise

Set up your Facebook page, separate to your personal profile. Link it to your Twitter account. Add a banner photo and a personal profile. Write a few words about this Facebook page so that people know what to find there. Join NetworkedBlogs (networkedblogs.com) and set your blog up on it so that it automatically posts to Facebook.

Pinterest

Pinterest is the new guy on the social-media block but has rapidly become extremely popular. It's rather like the scrapbooking craze, except people can do this digitally. You don't even have to be very creative – you can create an online following just by pinning other people's creative work and by having good taste. So do start a Pinterest account and build some Pinterest boards. Some bloggers say that much of their traffic is driven by Pinterest. I use Pinterest to create mood boards and idea boards. I don't so much follow Pinterest personalities as search for subjects that I'm interested in.

HOW TO GET KNOWN ON PINTEREST

- Join collaborative boards which are popular – this is a way of getting discovered. Join some in different countries. After a while you could ask for an invite to the board. I've joined vegan and vegetarian Pinterest boards all over the world because that kind of food interests me.
- Make it easy to pin your photos from your blog by adding the Pinterest button. In WordPress you can embed a Pinterest board on your blog.
- Post at different times to attract followers who live in different time zones: 11 a.m. for the UK and 3 a.m. for the United States.
- There are Pinterest workshops that study what elements will make your Pinterest board popular such as keywords, shape of image, type of image.
- Give your Pinterest images interesting descriptions using hashtags that will enable searches.
- Follow other Pinteresters. Some will follow back.
- Holidays such as Christmas and Halloween are a great time to pin inspirational images centred around that subject.
- Link your Pinterest boards with your other social media sites.
- Post both original images and curate other people's images.
- Pinterest now has analytics so you can find out more about what is popular.
- Now Pinterest has private boards. I've used these when working on projects such as the photo shoot for my book *V is for Vegan* (2015). This was shared with the food stylist, the prop stylist, the photographer and the art director. We could all pin inspirational images in the run-up to the photo shoots but were able to keep the project secret until the book came out.

Snapshot exercise

Set up your Pinterest account. Start five boards on subjects of your choice (e.g. Indian food, Valentine's Day food, barbecue recipes, kitchens I like, light lunches).

Instagram

I love Instagram because my background is in photography. I think visually so this is a social media app that I can get down with. The only irritating things about Instagram are the hashtags. People use up to 30 hashtags per photo all claiming to be #photooftheday, #picoftheday and other boasts. Call me old fashioned but as an Englishwoman I find this unseemly. Ideally, the most hashtags you should have is five but tests have shown that the more hashtags you use the more followers you will get. (Remember that you are largely competing with teenagers, rather than people with great photography skills.) Therefore they love anything on pop stars, nails, beauty and pouting duck-face selfies while on a beach or in a bar. You don't have to do this but I have noticed that selfie Instagrams tend to get liked. (Tap the pictures twice to do a shortcut 'like'.) Try to 'ride' hashtags that already exist on Instagram for your chosen subject.

Some vocabulary for the digital age

melfie: a male selfie

photobomb: when you jump into someone else's shot

selfie: a picture of yourself, preferably with a celebrity. You have an innate 'selfie' advantage if you have long arms, so now 'selfie sticks' are sold so that people can take selfies from beyond the normal range of the human arm.

shelfie: a picture of your bookshelf

welfie: 1) a wedding selfie or 2) someone who takes a lot of selfies

Some tips for Instagram:

- Use the site Iconosquare.com for analytics of which Instagrams do best.
- Put all your hashtags, bar a couple, on your second comment, not your first.

- Use geotagging – this attracts followers in the neighbourhood, rather like Foursquare.
- Use tags by tapping on the Instagram; it's like Facebook – you can tag people in the photo.

Instagram has some cool filters and frames that you can play around with to improve your photography, although some of them have become quite clichéd. As mentioned later in Chapter 9 on photography, you can use other apps as well to edit and upload your images, which you can mix and match with Instagram. You can also use video on Instagram, which has the same filters as the still photos. Instagram works well with Facebook and, since being bought by the former, is now trying to be a visual Facebook. The best time to Instagram is between 5 and 6 p.m.

A recent phenomenon is Instagram foodie stars, for instance @clerkenwellboy, who has over 60,000 followers. He started out working in the City and had the money to spend on posh restaurants, which he Instagrammed. Instagram picked up on him, featured him and almost overnight he accrued thousands of followers. Now every restaurant PR has him on its invite list. Clerkenwellboy doesn't need to blog; he just snaps and hashtags. He's at every foodie event, has featured in the *Evening Standard* and is now on Jamie Oliver's FoodTube.

A few chefs are complaining about people photographing their food. These chefs are crazy: people taking pictures of their food are advertising their restaurants for free. I've noticed, however, that the one type of social media that chefs like and make time for is Instagram. Chefs often think visually and want to share photos of how they have plated up their food. There is even a restaurant in South Africa that has a special light box where you can take your dinner and photograph it.

Instagram has definitely influenced photography in general. Owing to the physical limitations of a smartphone or tablet, many Instagrams are taken overhead, especially of food. This suits flatter food such as pizza and gives a graphic look to dishes.

If you want to be featured on the front page of Instagram, you can email Instagram@Instagram.com and ask to be on the suggested users list. It may work!

Snapshot exercise

Set up an Instagram account using the same name as your Twitter and Facebook page. Upload a picture, write a short biography, link it to Facebook. Take your first Instagrams, playing with the filters and the other tools on there.

Google Plus

At the moment Google Plus is a mess. Everyone seems to have several Google Plus accounts and are terrified to delete any of them. I've got three. I tried deleting one, which didn't work. One of them, which has no followers, is connected to my YouTube channel (now owned by Google). I don't know how to disconnect it from my YouTube channel so I'm considering deleting the channel.

I think Google Plus is trying to be the new Facebook. The thing is, we already have Facebook. The cool thing about Google Plus, probably the only cool thing at present, is Google Hangouts, which is a video or a group video, streamed via your webcam, over the Internet, rather like filming a Skype conversation.

Still, as Dan Toombs of The Curry Guy says, it's not going to go away, so sign up and try to use it as effectively as you can. Maybe one day Google will get it right. Already it has changed its policy to allow people to use their brand name rather than their real name, which is a step forward for those of us who have a separate brand (e.g. MsMarmitelover rather than Kerstin Rodgers).

Other platforms

You may find the following platforms useful. Explore them and see whether they will suit your needs.

LinkedIn: social networking for businesses (I've never found it useful).

Foursquare: a social network based on geographical position.

Klout: rates your social media importance.

Vine: enables you to shoot short videos. Instagram now has a video element too. Vine links well with Twitter while Instagram links well with Facebook.

Ning: enables you to build your own mini Facebook-type community. I use it for my Find A Supperclub site (supperclubfangroup.ning.com).

Meetup: a place where you can set up meetings. It's useful for meeting others with the same interests though you can also use it to create events that you charge for.

Snapchat, Whatsapp and (in China) **Tencent QQ:** instant messaging apps particularly used by teenagers and young adults.

Weibo (a Chinese Twitter equivalent) and **Orkut** (ditto for India): social media platforms that are popular in other countries. I started to get a ton of traffic from China and realized that it was because a microblogger on Weibo, a famous foodie in China, had recommended my site.

Digg, Stumbleupon and **Reddit:** social bookmarking sites (sites that enable users to bookmark and disseminate Internet media).

Tumblr: like Pinterest, a content producer and social bookmarking site distributing content from across the web.

Flickr: a photography community and place to store your photos.

Britmums and **Mumsnet:** blogging communities and forums for mothers who blog. They can give you help if you get stuck: on getting hosted, tips, design.

WordPress forums: these can also give help.

Urban Spoon: a social community for restaurant lovers.

Other ways of marketing your food writing

Attend blogging conferences and events and meet other people. Go to bloggers' events and be nice to bloggers. Yes, being popular as a human being is rather helpful, even in this digital arm's-length-contact age.

Go armed with cards. MOO does economical and stylish business cards. Always carry a few – you never know who you will meet.

Key idea

Good news! More people see your social media posts than you realize – in fact, ten times more than the people who actually comment or interact. You have a huge invisible audience.

Another way of making sure that people know about your food writing is to employ good SEO techniques. Make sure that they can find you. Dan Toombs, The Curry Guy who we met in Chapter 1, has some great tips. (They are worth following – he has 50,000 followers on Twitter!)

- **Make sure that your title includes the keyword/keyword phrase you are trying to be found for on Google.** For example, a pizza blog might want to be found for 'Sicilian-Style Pizza'. A possible recipe title might be 'Sicilian-Style Pizza – Salami and Garlic'.

- **Be sure to mention the keyword phrase several times in your post.** You should also highlight the phrase once in bold, once in italics and perhaps even one more time underlined. The phrase should be mentioned at least once in your opening paragraph. However, only write the keyword phrase if it reads well in your text. Don't 'keyword stuff'. Mention the phrase too many times and you could do more harm than good.

- **If possible, highlight your keyword phrase using 'H1', 'H2' and 'H3' title tags.** (In Blogger this is to be found under the box with the word 'Normal'. Underneath you will find 'header' 'subheading' and 'minor heading'.) You can really only do this in a long post or it looks like you're 'keyword stuffing'. (You've probably seen this, when a blog post looks very commercial and like a hard sell with lots of phrases in bold.)

- **Give each page a unique title.** This is easily done in WordPress; Blogger does this automatically. Use your keyword phrase as close to the beginning of the title as possible. Using the pizza example above, you could write something like 'Sicilian-Style Pizza – A Fantastic Salami and Garlic Pizza'.

- **Fill in a good description.** The description tag does not affect how you rank in Google but it could entice people to click through to your post. Something like 'I hope you love this Sicilian-style pizza as much as my family and I do. It is so good.

Wait until you try the crust!' would work. (In Blogger this description is on the sidebar named 'Search Description'.)

- **Do not fill in the keyword meta tags.** Many people still do this. It is frowned upon by Google and could negatively affect how your site ranks.
- **Be sure to add at least one link to another post on your site within each and every blog post.** The above Sicilian-style pizza post could link to a recipe for a special pizza sauce or an alternative crust, for example. (It's also good to link to each site: generosity is rewarded on Google.)
- **Use good-quality photos and be sure to label them.** Explain what is in the photograph so that Google and Bing know what is in the picture. Both search engines are giving better rankings to bloggers who use quality photographs and videos. It's a must! (On Blogger, you can label your photographs by clicking on the photo and opening the 'Properties' box. Then fill in the 'Alt Text' box with the description of your photo.)
- **If you have not already done so, open a Google Plus account and link your blog to your profile.** This helps Google recognize you as the author of the post. This is becoming increasingly important. There are a lot of good step-by-step instruction videos on setting up Google Authorship on YouTube.
- **Be social!** This is offsite stuff but if you aren't taking advantage of Twitter, Facebook, Pinterest, Google Plus and the others, you need to be. It would be too time-consuming for most people to be active in each social network. Find the ones you like and stay active. Also, be sure to make it easy for people to share your articles and follow you with the appropriate Social Share and Follow icons.

Next step

In Chapter 8 we will look at how to photograph and style food.

8

How to take great photographs of food

Illustrating a piece is vital. A picture tells a thousand words. Publishers are more likely to sign you if you are a good photographer – they may not have to fork out for one.

A short history of food photography

Food photography can range from brightly lit, functional pack shots, to the most gorgeous 'eat with your eyes' aspirational lifestyle pictures. Post-war food photography was elaborate and brightly coloured with fancy over-the-top food styling. Think Fanny Cradock and her bright-green mashed potatoes!

The history of food photography is also the history of technology and of homeware styles. Up until the 1960s, most cookery books used hand-drawn illustrations with the odd black-and-white food photograph. During the 1960s and 1970s food photographs tended to look like still lifes in paintings and were lit using tungsten lights that gave off warm spectrum lighting. Props were in earthy colours, and often in pottery or wood. This was the era of varnished chickens and ice cream made from flour and water. Hot lights meant food had to be faked to look good on camera.

In the late 1970s and early 1980s, flash lighting and colour photography were ubiquitous. Food photographs tended to be over-propped, with fantasy sets of lavish, aspirational luxury. Plates started to be modern and geometric – square, oblong and the fashionable hexagonal Eternal Beau plates. Food had to be perfect – not scruffy, no bites taken out of it, not a herb or a crumb out of place. After the Vaselined lenses and romantic blurriness of 1970s photos, 1980s photographs were highly focussed, very sharp, using glossy and gilt surfaces. Food illustration was a lifestyle indicator rather than having much to do with the food itself.

In the 1990s and the 2000s, the trend veered towards very natural, clean, bright, shallow depth-of-field photographs, very influenced by Donna Hay, the Australian cook and food stylist. The look favoured was 'white on white' with simple propping, maybe using some string or a bit of carefully crumpled artisanal paper wrapper. American lifestyle guru Martha Stewart very much copied Donna Hay's aesthetic. Increasingly, women were working and cooking, so food preparation and the way it was presented needed to be simpler, looser, more casual. Food shots contained minimal garnishing and a natural approach to making food, so burnt spots on a gratin would be left in. By now, everyone was shooting digitally and therefore shooting was cheaper. Chefs had started to come into food styling and they liked white, clean plates. The focus was on food, the beauty of ingredients, raw and cooked. Extreme close-ups, using a macro lens, were also coming to the fore.

From 2010 on is the era of hipster food photography, using Instagram and apps that give retro effects. Pictures are more rustic, gritty and authentic. At the moment, people are imitating old styles of photography from scratched glass plates to 1970s Kodak moments. The Instagram influence on photography is clear, with graphic photography composed in a square rather than a rectangle and an overhead angle that flattens the picture. Rather like the 1980s, we have reverted to expounding certain picturesque lifestyles using detailed and evocative propping rather than concentrating on the food.

In complete contrast, the food photography in the seminal cookbook *Modernist Cuisine* by Nathan Myhrvold used highly technical and futuristic photography techniques (no doubt courtesy of Photoshop) showing pressure cookers cut in half and jars full of vivid vegetables mid-boil – reminiscent of the work of artist Damian Hurst. There is nothing 'natural' about the photographs in this book: they resemble something from a science-fiction film, the food examined in microscopic detail.

Francine Matalon-Degni, food stylist

'But when all else fails, go back to the white plate.'

Here are some examples of food writers who take their own pictures:

- **Dan Lepard:** took the pictures for his book *Short and Sweet*.
- **Felicity Cloake:** *Guardian* recipe columnist who shoots her own photos.
- **Kerstin Rodgers (me!):** trained as a photographer, starting out in music, working for the *NME* and record companies (kerstinrodgers.com), moving on to portraits, fashion and

reportage. In the last few years I've been mostly shooting food and travel. I shoot all the pictures for my blog and for most of my books.

Blogging is very picture-led so most bloggers are proficient photographers. Some of the most celebrated bloggers have either a graphics or photographic background. It immediately gives them a leg-up on their competitors. Examples are:

- **What Katie ate:** Katie Quinn Davies is an Australian food writer, blogger, photographer and stylist who creates incredibly stylish work, with a strong 'dark and moody' style. www.whatkatieate.com
- **Miss Foodwise:** Belgian graphic designer, blogger and photographer Regula Lewin is obsessed with British food and culture. Her beautifully designed blog has perfectly composed and styled food photographs of historical British recipes. www.missfoodwise.com
- **Matt Bites:** American food blogger and author Matt Armendariz, shoots all his own work and gives photography classes. http://mattbites.com
- **La Tartine Gourmande:** French ex-pat food stylist and photographer Béatrice Peltre runs her beautiful food blog from Boston, USA. http://www.latartinegourmande.com
- **Cannelle et Vanille:** Ex-pat Basque Aran Goyoaga, a cookbook author, photographer and food stylist, now lives in the United States. http://www.cannellevanille.com

Good food photographers often earn more money than the writers.

Nowadays, the idea of following the written recipes of a historical cookbook writer such as Hannah Glasse, with vague quantities and devoid of photographs or even illustrations, defeats most of us. Gone are the days when Elizabeth David had a scratchy engraved drawing every few pages providing decoration but little instruction. Most of us like to have a photo of each recipe, so we know what the dish should look like. Since we can get much of our info online for free, cookery books are more like coffee table art books, beautiful, visually appealing objects that we can handle and admire. This has increased the importance of food photography.

Photographic step-by-step guides to a technique or recipe are always popular. Video is also a way of boosting visitors to your site: YouTube is one of the key ways to raise awareness of your 'brand'

and work. The modern food writer is expected to multi-task: you are not only expected to be able to cook well, but also to write, photograph, video and perform your recipes! The more of these skills you can master, the more chance of success you will have. Yes, there are still very grand old-style food writers who can pen a few choice paragraphs in the posh papers but, as a newbie to the scene, you are going to have to up your game.

So in this chapter, I'm going to give you a short but intense exploratory tour into the word of food photography and styling.

Equipment

Buy the best camera you can afford. You know all those brilliant photos in cookery books? Those photographers have fantastic cameras and pin-sharp lenses. You'd have to be an idiot to take bad pictures with them. On the other hand, equipment isn't everything. You can take great pictures with your phone or on a cheap amateur camera. If you've got style and a vision, the equipment doesn't matter quite so much.

At the upper end of the price scale:
Much of the fantastic food photography you see in books and magazines is shot with a Canon 5d, a nice heavy-weight professional bit of kit that can also shoot video. Some TV programmes are entirely shot on the Canon 5d.

The Canon 6d is very similar, but more lightweight and about a grand cheaper. I was so impressed that I bought this camera along with a macro 24–105mm lens.

Medium range:
If you just want a point-and-shoot, a handbag-sized Canon G12 is convenient as a second camera for carrying around and for trips. As well as being easy to use technically, it's also cheaper.

Lower end:
Don't forget your phone. You can take really excellent photos and short pieces of video on your phone camera. There are many apps you can use to transform and improve those pictures, so what you lack in expensive kit, you can make up for with artistry.

Buy a tripod. In the UK, at least, most of the year we have gloomy skies and a very short shooting window during winter. A decent tripod, easy to manipulate while shooting, allowing for smooth movements, will make shooting in low light a possibility. As a rule you can't hand-hold steadily if you are shooting at less than 1/60th of a second. I've just bought a Manfrotto Befree travel tripod. For shooting in restaurants you may want to get a small tabletop tripod which can be bought very cheaply.

It's true that a tripod restricts you. It's harder to be spontaneous about composition. In that case, move around without the tripod, get the best angle and then put the camera on the tripod.

Using a tripod will ensure that your photos are crisply in focus, with no camera shake. It also means you are hands-free and can, especially if you don't have a food stylist, step into the shot and make changes to the set-up whenever you want without losing your frame.

 Key idea

Do not get hung up on the equipment aspect. If you can afford good equipment, that's wonderful. But photographer Paul Winch-Furness told me that, in his photography classes, his students get amazing results just using household objects like bedside lamps for lighting. One girl even used sweet wrappers to make coloured filters for her lights and camera lenses!

Techniques

COMPOSITION
Crop

I'm fairly purist about cropping. It's good training to attempt to get the shot right in camera rather than relying on editing afterwards. The viewfinder in some cameras does not reflect accurately what you will get in the final picture, so check that. However, in food photography, cropping is acceptable. Sometimes just a section of the dish is more effective. But try to crop in the camera, not in the editing, and shoot tight.

Angle

Naturally, the angle you choose will depend on the food you are shooting and the container it is in. A tall stack of pancakes you will want to shoot from a low angle from the side. A plate of pasta in a bowl you might want to choose a 45-degree angle, giving you a view of the pyramid of pasta, the sauce and the bowl it came in. Pizzas you will probably want to shoot overhead.

- **Shoot close:** we want to see oozing and shine and texture and drips. We want to feel like we could pick it up and eat it.
- **Shoot low:** at fork level. Especially if it's tall food, then we want to see the layers.
- **Shoot overhead:** this gives an instant graphic look and works well for flat food such as pizzas.

The classic food photo angle is 30 to 45 degrees overhead, giving you an overview of the food and a bit of the bottom of the plate/bowl.

Framing

Compose the picture in thirds: this is known as the 'rule of thirds'. Break the picture down into thirds both horizontally and vertically. If you can imagine this as a grid on your image, then place anything of interest on the intersectional points of the grid. One's eye naturally follows the intersectional points. For instance, the line of the horizon should be on the line where the horizontal thirds lie: one-third up or two-thirds up. Another thing in the West we tend to do is look at the right side first then go to the left. Things of visual interest are best placed on the right. It's the same with book design: place the photo on the right-hand page and the written text on the left.

If using your photographs on a blog, it's easier to shoot everything landscape. That way all of your photos will align. Books are normally shot as a vertical, upright portrait picture.

EXPOSURE

You need to master some technical stuff to improve your photography. If you are using an SLR, what I would like you to do is to wean yourself off the auto mode: to stop using the auto button and start focusing and exposing your photos manually.

Different photographers have different styles but you should at the beginning aim for a correct exposure. Remember it's easier to lighten an underexposed picture than add detail to an overexposed shot. So I tend to shoot slightly under.

There are two main factors in exposure: shutter speed and aperture. Shutter speed is classically measured using this sequence:

8 seconds	½ second
4 seconds	¼ ⅛ $\frac{1}{15}$ $\frac{1}{30}$ $\frac{1}{60}$ $\frac{1}{125}$ $\frac{1}{250}$
2 seconds	$\frac{1}{500}$ $\frac{1}{1000}$
1 second	

Aperture generally follows this sequence:

1.4	8
2.0	11
2.8	16
4	22
5.6	

Photographers call these 'F/stops' or just 'stops'.

The aperture is the 'hole' the lens shutter makes when taking a picture, letting light through. The bigger the 'hole', the more light. The speed is how long or short this 'hole' is open for. The longer the shutter speed (8 seconds is clearly longer than a 1/1000th of a second), the more light and the brighter your picture.

Play with under- and overexposing by setting the needle on the exposure up to one stop above the 'zero' mark, or one stop under (also called 'bracketing your exposures'). Work towards using Manual rather than Automatic. Focus manually and set the exposure manually.

If you are in a situation where you don't have time to fiddle with settings, then, by all means, shoot on automatic.

FOCUS AND DEPTH OF FIELD

What is a depth of field? A long depth of field is when you shoot a photo and both the front and the back are in focus. A short depth of field is when only a small portion of the composition is sharp. Small apertures (counter-intuitively these are apertures with higher numbers such as 11 or 22) give a long depth of field; wider, bigger apertures (with smaller numbers such as 2.8 or 4) produce a short depth of field.

> ## Key idea
>
> Try to focus on the frontal part of the food or whatever is the 'star' ingredient.

Bokeh is not a dubious sexual practice but a Japanese word for the blurry 'noise' which occurs when you are using a short depth of field. Many photographers try to get good 'bokeh' shapes, especially in the macro or very close-up photography that is necessary for food.

In a shot of a dish of, say, potato salad with a short depth of field, the very centre is sharp and the rest is blurry. A long depth of field would mean that all of the potatoes would be in focus.

LIGHTING AND COLOUR TEMPERATURE

The most important element of photography is light – effectively, you are painting with light. Great light will transform the most mundane of still lifes. In terms of colour temperature, you generally want food to be on the warmer end of the scale. It's supposed to look appetising and homely, not cold and harsh. So while you should feel free to get arty with your food pictures, the ultimate goal is to make them look *tasty*.

A key concern is the 'white balance': you'll have this in the menu of most cameras. If you aren't using automatic, you will need to set it to either: daylight, cloudy, tungsten, neon light or custom.

Even if you mostly shoot on automatic, try to learn manual because it is particularly useful for when you don't have much light – for example, shooting your meal in a restaurant. Sometimes the automatic will correct the light sufficiently but I've often noticed it is better if you set the white balance to say 'tungsten' (which is good for candles and ordinary light bulbs) or even 'custom'.

For the custom setting, focus your camera on a plain, white surface in the light conditions that you intend to shoot in, and press the custom setting button. This will set the white balance. But do have a look at the results, compare and contrast. Go with whichever white balance looks best to you and what reflects the scene best.

Use natural light. I hate studio lighting with food – it makes it look synthetic and old-fashioned. You have to be really skilful to avoid that. Also, try not to use flash. Flash removes all of the atmosphere.

Sometimes food is best shot against the light. This will show the texture and you can use reflectors to bounce back the light on to the dark side. You can make reflectors for bouncing light towards the shadowy side from white boards, tin foil or black boards that add a lovely dark edge. You can make these yourself just by painting a large cardboard box or covering it with foil. Or you can buy a Lastolite, which is a foldable small reflector. The white transparent version can also be used as a diffuser when there is very bright sunlight.

Don't shoot, if you can avoid it, at midday, certainly in summer. The best light is morning (a blue light) or just before dusk (a warm light).

Make sure, when you are taking pictures, that all the lights are switched off, especially strip lighting, which has an awful green colour. You want a good 'white balance' whereby you are attempting to achieve a neutral white colour for the whites in your photo.

If the colour looks wrong, shoot in different modes until you find the colour that best reflects your vision of the picture:

- **Tungsten light** (ordinary light bulbs): gives off an orangey light so the tungsten white balance setting will cool it, making it bluer.
- **Fluorescent/strip light:** gives off a greenish light so the fluorescent setting will correct that and give a whiter, more magenta colour.
- **Candlelight:** orangey, warm.
- **Daylight:** depends on what time of day.
- **Early morning:** bluish light.
- **Midday:** harsh white light.
- **Early evening:** warm orangey light.

You can manually adjust the white balance in your camera but 'auto' will do it automatically for you.

Sometimes it's good to shoot against the light, for instance, if you want to highlight the texture and sheen. So try shooting from the 'wrong' side.

Props and styling

We've all heard about food photography tricks such as varnishing chicken and using shaving cream as cream. There is also the trick about putting a microwaved tampon in the food to create steam. I've never met anyone who has done this, but perhaps it works. Some cakes in baking books are done with decorated polystyrene models, which is why the sides and angles are so straight and neat.

Here, though, are some key tips that really do work:

- **First of all, tidy up.** There is no point beautifully cooking and arranging a plate of food complete with artistic props and then shooting it against a background of mess. Remove any rubbish from the background. Great props can help tell the story of the dish but don't over-prop. Instead...

- **Introduce texture into your props:** the metallic sheen of cutlery, the gleam of china, the webbing of a tablemat or linen napkin, a wooden bowl. Start collecting different kinds of cutlery, plates, bowls, napkins, cake stands and so on.

- **Use hands.** A worn pair of hands rolling out dough or a small child's little paw cupping a bowl or a hand with brightly painted fingernails holding a lurid cocktail can add humanity and a background story to a photo.

- **Think about what you are presenting food on.** Most food is arranged on a round plate: the frame within the frame. Try to use other devices for presenting food: on a wooden board, on a stone, nestled among plants. Keep looking for good bits of background: an old chopping board, some greaseproof paper, a cooking rack. Use wallpaper, wrapping paper, tea towels and different tablecloths.

  I recently painted some cheap wooden chopping boards in different colours with paint testers. You can get an aged shabby-chic effect by painting a strong base colour in emulsion, then rubbing the corners, edges and small areas with a wax candle when the paint is dry. Then, using emulsion paint in white, lightly paint over the strong base colour and waxy areas. Let it dry, then rub lightly with some sandpaper. The wax will come off, letting the base colour shine through.

- **Consider colour.** Food looks great shot on a turquoise or bluey green background as most food is warm coloured – yellows, browns, oranges, reds. Think of complementary colours: orange/blue; red/green; yellow/violet.
- **It's easier to photograph food when it's cold.** It's also easier to photograph certain types of food, for instance salad or desserts or cakes. A Victoria sponge has more visual appeal than a stew.
- **Show the ingredients that go into the dish.** These can be added to the composition, to demonstrate the steps involved.

 Key idea

As a general rule, make sure that you shoot quickly. Food rarely improves if kept hanging about. This is especially true if it's a hot dish. You are looking for spontaneity and a natural quality in food photography.

Food styling tools

Tweezers: You'll need these to tease food into shape, pick up the odd stray herb or seed, or reach into something that you don't want to spoil with your fingers. Remember, if you are taking close-ups then you need to be detail-obsessed.

Super-absorbent towels: to prevent the rest of the 'set' getting splashed when pouring; to mop up drips and puddles if the food has sat there too long; to clean your hands; to dry props.

Cotton buds: to clean spots or spatters that you haven't intended.

Toothpicks and skewers: to prop up food or to stitch things together, such as a banana leaf parcel containing baked fish.

Lego bricks: Being small these are easy to hide when used to tilt small pieces of food towards the camera.

Spray bottle containing water and glycerine (with fine mist option): Using this can liven up food, making it look moist and edible. It can add shine and sparkle.

- **Season from a height.** You will have seen Jamie Oliver and others sprinkling salt and oil from a great height. This isn't just for showmanship; it also means that the seasoning is spread evenly.

- **Green it up.** Keep back some fresh herbs to scatter, depending what is in the dish. To make salad and herbs look fresh, plunge them into ice-cold water for 15 minutes prior to shooting. Then dry them carefully on kitchen towel.

- **Use lime and lemon wedges** (where appropriate to the dish). These will add colour and freshness. The same goes for chillies and spring onions. Cut spring onions at an angle – it's more stylish.

- **Rip bread rather than slice it.**

- **Use oil.** Brush on oil to ingredients that have been sitting around and starting to wilt. For instance, I shot a chicken tagine when it came out of the oven. Ten minutes later, the chicken started to look dull. I brushed some vegetable oil on to the skin, and instantly it had that 'just out of the oven' look.

- **Use some of the ingredients that you used to make the dish.** For instance, if you have made a cup of hot chocolate with a sprinkling of nutmeg, place a small nutmeg grater and a nutmeg next to the hot chocolate.

- **Dust it!** Use a tea strainer to sprinkle a little icing sugar, flour or cocoa powder (which also covers any problems with the food). This gives the picture some movement.

- **Open up the food.** Photograph the complete dish then take a bite with a fork or carve a slice or break off a piece.

- **Add crumbs and drips.** Such details make people salivate – you want the shots to look almost as if someone was halfway through eating it. Food photography shouldn't be too 'clean'; it should look alive. Droppers can be used to add a last-minute drip to a shot.

- **Use parchment paper, doilies or a crumpled brown paper bag to make things look casual but chic.**
- **Keep portions small.** Like people, objects put on weight in the camera lens. Large mounds of food can look overwhelming and off-putting. For example, if your recipe is for four people, have a small portion on a plate, with a fork, and the rest behind and out of focus. This also means that small forks/knives/spoons and plates are very useful for plating up these small portions of food.

Post-production

Post production is your chance to further improve your images. As I said, try to get focus, exposure and crop right when you're taking the photographs. However, the editing process is also important.

I don't have great software, I use iPhoto and Snapseed. If you have Lightroom or Photoshop and you can use it, fantastic. The first thing I do is narrow the 'levels' on iPhoto, by dragging in the markers either side. Then I try to balance the colour – not too warm, not too cold. I sharpen a little, increase definition.

In Snapseed, for photos that are landscapes or objects rather than people, I often use the 'drama' filter.

If you are a blogger, shrink your pictures when you upload them. This makes them harder to steal and your site will load more quickly. Do watermark using picmonkey.com.

Only post your best pictures. Don't use too many photos of the same thing but at marginally different angles. So many food blogs do this, but I don't really understand why. It points to a weakness in editing and makes the blogger look a bit stupid and empty-headed.

Ideally, you should test your site on different browsers (Safari etc.) to see how long your blog takes to load. Always check how a blog reads on your phone after posting.

If you have several photos that aren't pin-sharp, display in a collage. Free online sites like picmonkey.com are a great way to do easy collages. You can add frames and edit pictures also.

APPS FOR CAMERA PHONES/IPHONEOGRAPHY

You can take fantastic pictures using the camera on your smartphone. The BBC now trains all of its reporters to take pictures and video on smartphones to save money on camera crews and photographers. One of the advantages of a camera phone is that you can photograph things more easily without being seen and also subjects are less spooked.

If using a phone camera, then it's often better to use an iPhone torch rather than the flash facility on the camera.

I'm assuming you have downloaded the free app 'Instagram'. Once you have mastered/played around with all the filters and frames on Instagram, you can explore other photo apps.

You can do a thing called 'stacking the apps' where you run a photo through one or more apps before sharing it on Instagram. Here is a list of a few of these apps (there are new ones appearing all the time):

- **Hipstamatic:** has lots of filters. 'Dream Canvas' is a favourite film to use, with painterly edges. 'Oggl' gives you access to Hipstamatic filters and is good to use with an iPad.
- **Snapseed:** the drama filter is great with clouds. I use this app a great deal.
- **TouchRetouch:** helps you easily remove unwanted content from your photos.
- **Image Blender:** adds layers and masks to your photos.
- **360 Panorama:** enables a panorama that is good for big rooms. This function is now part of the iPhone6.
- **Noir:** enables your pictures to be turned into black and white.
- **Vignette:** is the Android version of Hipstamatic – tilt/shift is good.
- **Colour Splash:** gives you black and white with a bit of colour.
- **Actionshot:** a free app that takes seven frames of something moving and then blends those frames for a final image.
- **Filterstorm Neue:** sophisticated software for iPhoneographers with curves, masks, saturation, tiling, advanced export formats.
- **decim8:** takes a picture, chops it up, and rearranges.

Make sure that you buy apps on your computer, then you can plug in your phone or your tablet without having to pay for each device.

Role models

Look at other people's work. You can learn most by looking. A great writer must read, a great photographer or artist must look. Here are a few UK-based food photographers who I admire:

- **Jean Cazals:** creates lovely dark textural photos. I love this guy's work. He won best photographer in the Pink Lady Apple food photography awards in 2012.
- **Jason Lowe:** has a great feel for light, and is particularly good at reportage. He shot my first book.
- **David Loftus:** shoots energetic, beautifully composed pictures and is Jamie Oliver's photographer of choice.
- **Keiko Oikawa:** creates very feminine, detailed, whimsical pictures.
- **Yuki Sugura:** quirky and creative and uses some avant-garde techniques; again, has a soft feminine approach.
- **Jan Baldwin:** creates images with colourful, strong composition.
- **Paul Winch-Furness:** started out photographing food in restaurants and has now progressed to shooting books. He has a reportage style, likes to include the surroundings and create an ambiance. He's also a flattering photographer for chefs such as myself, without resorting to Photoshop.

Don't just stick to food. Many of my influences and favourite photographers such as Tim Walker, Sarah Moon and Sebastião Salgado work in other fields such as fashion or reportage.

Key idea

Be realistic: professional food photographers have a big team of helpers. Apart from the photographer, you'd have an assistant or two, a food stylist, a home economist, someone preparing the food, a props person, an art director, someone doing post-production… You probably don't have that. Nevertheless, food bloggers manage to get very good results.

Workshop 1

Try photographing food, let's say a composed salad:

- on a white plate
- on a patterned plate
- on a dark plate.

Then with each option, shoot from above, at fork level and at a 45-degree angle.

Again with each option, shoot from the direction of the light, shoot against the light, shoot with a lamp (this could be a desk lamp or a light bulb, whatever you have to hand).

Then shoot each option with a light background, with a dark background, then with a patterned or textural background.

Have a good look at the resulting photographs. What works best? What do you prefer?

Workshop 2

Figure out the best place in your flat or house to photograph your food.

Look for the best light and the best background. At what time of day is the light good?

Try photographing food on differently shaped, sized or coloured plates. Look at your cutlery and napkins. What range of colours and styles do you have? Are the tablecloths attractive? Are the tea napkins washed and ironed?

Edit exercise

Shoot a plate of spaghetti. With a fork, twirl the pasta into attractive shapes on the plate. Then do an exposure exercise: try overexposing, underexposing and shooting at the 'correct' exposure. What do you think?

 ## Robert Capa, Magnum photographer

'If your pictures aren't good enough, you aren't close enough.'
[OK, this quote is about war photography, not snapping your dinner. But you get the picture. Close-ups of food really work.]

Next step

In Chapter 9 we look at the important issue of how to earn money from your food writing.

9

Earning money

In this chapter we will look at ways of (a horrible phrase I know) 'monetizing' your food writing.

It's important.

Money, money, money

The whole 'writing for free' thing is a big problem: increasingly, even professional journalists don't get paid. Print media is in a bind, budgets are squeezed and internships, where people can get work experience possibly leading to jobs, tend to be awarded to those who are well connected. This has led to a narrowing of talent in journalism and writing in general.

Publications like *The Huffington Post* rely on unpaid writers to provide content. This caused ructions when the owner, Arianna Huffington, then sold the site for millions of dollars. It seemed very unfair.

Know your worth

One of the first tasks is summoning up the courage to charge for what you love doing. It's about knowing your worth. As a freelancer, you have to balance the free work to increase your 'profile' with what you need in order to live.

Whether to do work for free to benefit your 'profile' is a judgement call. If you are starting out as a blogger and a famous company asks you to give them a recipe for free, you may wish to consider that.

It's not worth it when you get an email (as I once did) from a little-known cruise company asking you to write for its website. 'What's the fee?' I asked. 'Nothing,' came the reply, 'but it'll be good for your profile.' I looked at the website, which nobody ever reads – it's a bog-standard, content-light, commercial website for a cruise company. They weren't even offering me a cruise! This is known as trying it on. I'd be very surprised if anyone said yes.

So, as well as drawing up the courage to charge for something you may have hitherto considered a hobby, you need to learn to say no.

On your site/blog, have a media pack. This is a statement of what you will do and won't do. Include information such as: how long you have been blogging; how much you charge; your skills and areas of interest; what you can do for them. Have a rate for your writing, for your photography, for your videos, for your recipes (with and without photos), for your food styling, for your cooking demonstrations, for your cooking, for your public talks.

For instance, I was asked by a digital PR company whether I would participate in a workshop in which professionals would ask me about my work as a blogger. It was a commercial company and I charged them.

If a brand, restaurant, food producer or PR company asks you to give them advice, this is consultancy and you should not do it for free.

Key idea

Have a look at 'Stop working for free' on Facebook. This is a group where freelancers from all categories of work – artists, writers, photographers, videographers – share their experiences and frustrations.

Pitching

This is scary stuff. I still get very nervous pitching, even though it's just an email. The worst part is when someone completely blanks you. Sometimes it's even people you know.

So I sought the expertise of Katy Salter.

Katy Salter used to work for Waitrose Food Illustrated *and is now freelance. She works for* The Guardian *and* Delicious *among others. Like many food journalists, she also has a well-respected food blog. Her first book,* Dairy-Free Delicious, *will be published in 2015 by Quadrille.*

What kind of articles or subjects tend to do well?

Food topics with a timely/newsworthy hook, that is, something that gives an editor a pressing reason to publish now. So, that could be a trend that's really taking off with a new product or restaurant opening, a food shortage, a story that ties into a new book or TV show, or something that follows on from a big story in the press. Subjects that get people talking also do well as does anything about finding the perfect or definitive version of something – Felicity Cloake's 'Perfect' series for *The Guardian* is a perfect example of this. Remember that magazines work much further ahead than papers and websites.

Have you any dos and don'ts for pitching? When is a good time? Who should one write to?

Always read the publication you're pitching to first! It sounds obvious but you'd be surprised how many people don't. Instead of a generic idea, think about how it will work in the specific sections of the site/magazine/paper – for example, does the magazine always have a 'meet the producer' slot about farmers and food producers that they always commission out to freelancers? If so, see what they've already covered and pitch some new ideas that work for that section. Editors will love you if you make their life easier.

Personally, as a features editor, I always preferred emails to phone calls and that's something I now stick to as a freelance writer – less chance of catching someone at a bad time. But if you've got the gift of the gab by all means call a commissioning editor direct – just get to the point quickly, only pitch one killer idea and don't be surprised if they're a bit grumpy! Lots of titles have morning features or ideas meetings so I'd say late morning, early in the week was as good a time to call as any, but there's no hard and fast rule. Otherwise, send a polite and friendly email outlining your idea. Don't send written articles as almost all editors want to commission according to the tone, formats and word counts of their title. Pitch to the features or commissioning editor, or relevant section editor if it's a newspaper or website.

What do you do if you don't hear back?

Follow up with another polite and friendly email a week later. Be keen but not stalkerish! Once you've got the commission, obviously one should stick to the word count.

Any other advice?

Yes – stick to the brief! Plus, always file on time – again, you'd be surprised how many people don't. If you stick to the word count (or only go slightly over at least), file on time and cover all the points the editor has asked you to in the brief, editors will love you.

If somebody asks you to write for free, what would your advice be?

All the major newspapers and magazines pay writers, with some exceptions, for their blog sections. Personally, I feel very strongly that the only writing you should do for free should be your own blog, which is a great way of both showcasing and honing your writing. Don't believe people who tell you a free article is 'great exposure' – your blog can potentially get you much more exposure (and revenue) than 200 words in a free arts mag with no budget. Even a very modest fee is better than nothing.

The fewer people who agree to write for free, the more titles will have to continue paying professional writers what they're worth and the longer it can remain a viable (if very competitive) career. Think about this carefully if you're in it for the long haul. That said, if it's a really high-profile opportunity and you really are just starting out, then it could be worth doing. Just remember, if people know you write for free, it's going to be harder to get them to pay you further down the line!

Monetizing your blog

Brands are looking for influence via Google, Twitter and other social media. So, once you get going, you will receive a stream of unsolicited emails from PRs and marketing departments. In fact, you will receive so many, you will feel like you are very busy and important. But beware. These PRs will waste your time and energy and bend your blog to their timetable and their messages.

You need to decide what kind of blog you want:

- Is it to earn money? Then consider the 'monetized' route.
- Is it to get more writing work or a book deal? In that case, be very careful about getting sucked into the commerciality of it. Your content will suffer.
- Is it to finally have a place, your place, where you can express yourself? Or a combination of the above motivations? Then consider carefully the balance of your free content versus paid content.

Directly, you can make money in the following ways:

GOOGLE ADS

These make very little money, around £30 to £50 every few months if you have a popular blog. Is it worth it having those ads cluttering up your blog? The ads can sometimes feature inappropriate content. One blogger, LavenderCooks, told me readers were writing to her and saying that her Google ads were sometimes pornographic. She couldn't see that on her blog but when she went abroad and accessed her blog, she could see this for herself. You don't really want porn on a baking blog, so she removed the ads.

SPONSORED POSTS

This is where a brand or product ask you to either write about its product or asks you to 'host' a competition to win their product on your blog. 'Native advertising' is another term for sponsored posts. This comes under Office of Fair Trading (OFT) regulations. Just as advertising in conjunction with print media has to be labelled 'advertorial', sponsored posts have to be clearly marked 'in collaboration with'.

 Key point

Brands will do anything not to have a post say it is sponsored. They will even pay cash so that the fact that you've been paid does not go on the books.

You can charge between £50 and £350 for this, depending on the popularity and influence of your blog. I think it goes without saying that you would only do this for products you actually use and approve of. I've been offered a great deal of money to publicize products I don't like. I've said no. I was once in a PR's office tasting a cook-chill meal from a vegetarian food brand. It was so vile that I spat out the rubbery textured vegetable protein 'scampi' and turned down the deal. Which means I'm ethical but poor. Your choice.

However, a warning: Sally Whittle of foodies100.com believes that Google will start to clamp down on sponsored posts.

 Key idea

Charge more if you choose to take advantage of the money and work with brands you don't like.

OTHER WAYS TO MONETIZE YOUR BLOG

- Accept banner ads from a firm.
- Start an adjacent business and use your blog as a shop window for that business. This could be consultancy for brands, your

cooking classes, your food tour, your supper club, your street food business.

- Start an online shop, perhaps for your homemade products or for your deli.
- You could also sell merchandising linked to your blog.
- Hold food events. In my case, I run a supper club and various other events. This is the equivalent of a 'bricks and mortar' business. In the record business, nobody makes any money from recording anymore as it is all streamed for free. The only way musicians make money is through frequent touring. A live concert is something you cannot digitally replace. Happily, this is even more the case with food events. All the food blogging and writing and photographing and food telly in the world are not going to replace the actual real-life 3D reality of smelling, tasting, eating and drinking at a food event. Consequently, we have the invention of the 'pop-up' – a short-term part-time temporary restaurant/bar/food experience, which means that you don't have to endure the life-sapping commitment, not to mention financial cost, of a full-time restaurant.
- Start an actual restaurant. Most restaurants don't have blogs. Most people who work in restaurants don't have the time. But there are bloggers who have started restaurants and done very well. Probably the most famous example is Mikael Jonsson of Hedone, a Swedish food blogger who, dissatisfied with the quality of food he was eating in restaurants, decided to start his own. Within two years he had a Michelin star – but his blog is now closed.

Key idea

It's unrealistic to run a full-time restaurant and write. Some chefs undertake this challenge, even writing their own articles and books, like Rowley Leigh of Le Café Anglais, but they are few and far between. Usually, the most chefs can manage is Instagram and Twitter, although this tends to be the younger generation of chefs, such as Luke Robinson of Bonnie Gull (@Gullychef) restaurant.

There are subtler ways of monetizing: collaborations, limited editions, creating a flavour for the brand and other branded content.

How much to charge

Most mainstream publications will have a set rate of how much they pay. Obviously, if you have a world exclusive – say, Kate Middleton splurging ketchup down her front at a food truck – then the sky is the limit. But, generally, the rate for print media is higher than for online. You can check the standard rates on the National Union of Journalists (NUJ) website (www.nuj.org.uk).

For blogs, it depends on traffic and influence but:

- On average a sponsored post (with a tested recipe) would cost £300. If you are doing the photo, add more.
- A beginner blogger may earn around £40 for a post.
- For video: the rate is between £2,000 and £5,000.

You can also do adverts, for instance a display CPM. Thirty-five per cent goes to an agency such as Handpicked.com. If you are starting to build a name as a blogger, you need to negotiate with the brand exactly what they expect – how many blog posts, tweets, Instagrams, Pinterest boards and so on. If you are doing a bespoke article or campaign, negotiate a flat fee.

Should you work with an agency? This is an option open to you once you have built a following. An agency helps with maintaining a good relationship with a PR – you don't have to get your hands dirty by discussing the money stuff.

Some bloggers only do sponsored posts. Krista of Handpicked.com says this is a bad idea. Clients will refuse to work with a blogger who carries exclusively sponsored content. 'You need a healthy balance,' says Krista. 'I have bloggers that will refuse branded content work because they will say, oh last month, I posted too many sponsored posts, I need a break. They get flak from their readers …'

'My job', continues Krista, 'is to keep expectations real between bloggers and brands.'

 Key idea

Ensure that you do not only feature sponsored posts. Make sure that your blog is still your place to write. There is a huge value in reality, with real people – don't become a branded mouthpiece. It will devalue *your* brand.

A final word on sponsored posts: sometimes you get approached to write ridiculous things. One blogger I know was asked to write about bingo. She refused; it was not her brand. As you become a better-known blogger, you will get literally hundreds of emails a week and this can take up a great deal of your time. Nevertheless, try to reply politely to approaches. However, if there is no name on the email, don't reply. When you get an email where they don't address you, it's an anonymous mail-out. These you can ignore.

Monetizing your videos and YouTube content

It is possible to earn money from YouTube videos but you must set up an Adsense account. This enables a revenue split between you and YouTube. You can look at your ad performance report in YouTube analytics. But first of all, don't worry about monetization. You have to hone your skills first. You won't earn any money unless you get literally tens of thousands of views as payment is made per mille, known as RPM, or revenue per mille.

Interview: Neil Davey, freelance travel and food journalist; author of *The Bluffer's Guide*

> *Neil Davey is a blogger, journalist, pub quiz addict (he runs a food quiz) and author. He specializes in travel and food. He's a big lad – you can tell he loves eating, which is probably one of the best qualifications for being a food writer.*

How did you get into freelancing?

I worked in private banking for 11 years. I was very interested in films so I met a couple who ran a (now defunct) publication called *Footloose*. They suggested that I wrote film reviews for them. I started doing it for free. After a while, my wife told me to give up banking and do something I wanted to do. She was sick of living with a, and I quote, 'miserable bastard'. So, I resigned. This was a mistake. The first year, 1998, I earned precisely £45. In that year, I blew through my savings.

My first advice if you want to become a food writer is: take a part-time job. Because you need connections and I didn't have any.

Then, I had some luck. The assistant editor at *Footloose* was leaving and I took his job. I still wasn't getting paid but I did part-time work at the Royal Albert Hall, which was great fun – I met lots of resting musicians and actors. I also started to write restaurant reviews.

What did being an assistant editor teach you? Because you are seeing it from the other side, aren't you?

When I advertised for contributors to write about food, I got a thousand replies in a week. It took me a week to go through them.

Now, I know to ask people to supply raw copy. One guy sent me a piece that was published; it was very good. Then I got his raw, unedited copy. The guy couldn't spell or form a sentence. Basically, the subeditor had written it. It took me a long time to sort the piece out. As an editor that isn't worth your while.

Why did you move into food from doing showbiz and film?

In the 1990s, you'd get 20 minutes with a celebrity and that was OK – you could build some kind of rapport. Now, you get six minutes. It's not possible to write something good. But in the food world, people are so generous with their time: you can spend hours with them. Chefs invite you into their kitchens.

William Leigh, of The Boy Done Food blog (no longer going), suggested I do a blog. It was 2006 when I started Lambshank Redemption. It was supposed to be about film and food but it ended up as more about food. I've posted sporadically, actually I've posted more this year.

What do you think, having worked as both a blogger and a journalist, about the divisions between the two?

Blame for the state of journalism has been laid at the door of bloggers, it's not true. A lot of the snobbery of blogger vs. journalist has dissipated. The advantages of blogging are that it is much more immediate. Some companies avoid online but I think that's old-fashioned. I don't rip into bloggers; they are all writers. Some 'proper writers' I can't abide, for instance A.A. Gill. I can admire his writing, but I'd never go out of my way to read him.

Blogging has allowed people to talk about food. It has allowed a lot more people to have a voice. I like the food community. Bloggers

I like to read include Dan of Essex Eating and Food Urchin. Food Urchin is brilliant but I'd hate to have to edit him. It's sometimes 600 words before he gets on to the subject matter but that's the joy of a blog – you have space.

You only read men?

I also like Niamh of Eatlikeagirl.com. But with all these blogs, I don't read every post. I don't like bloggers who have a sense of self-importance.

What about the money? Do you ever write for free? Do you do sponsored posts?

Most people have started off writing for free. I'd say write for free for some publications. But, for instance, *Sainsbury's* magazine asked me as a blogger to write for free. At that point, it's a disadvantage to be seen as a blogger rather than a journalist. Yes, I've done the odd sponsored post for a product or brand that I like. Or sometimes it's payment in kind, which can work well. For instance, I did a car review when on a trip, which meant that I didn't have to hire a car. The value of the rental was worth more than I would have got from writing the piece.

Some publications haven't upped their freelance rates for six years. It's tough out there. You can get anything from 5p to £1 a word. There is more competition than there was five years ago.

How do you get work?

I'm always trying to find a new market. I find that all good things happen by chance but generally things happen when I got up off my arse and did shit. I'm a great believer in fate: you meet the right people at the right time. I do feel creepy schmoozing. But I play the long game.

Your tips for pitching?

It's generally sheer luck. As an editor, I'd call someone if their CV was on the top of the pile that day. And then they were the person to answer the phone or reply to the email. You have to maximize opportunities. It is all about relationships, but you can't force relationships.

Normally, I pitch to someone I've met. Maybe we've been out for dinner or for drinks or on a press do together. I follow up. I do a lot of networking on trips. I'll stay up late, have a drink with the others.

The two main things are relationships and persistence. Persistence is almost more important than talent; it's maybe 60/40.

If you get an opportunity, make the most of it. Editors move on. New people come in.

You never know who is going to end up where.

So Neil, to finish up, what is your dream job?

I'd love to do radio. I'm not that fussed about TV, the camera adds 10 pounds! I'd like to do more travel.

Every few years, I get together with friends and we look at our careers. We pick three or five targets that we want to achieve. Then, we meet and see if we've achieved our goals and, if we haven't, it's normally because we haven't had time. Usually, however, we do achieve our targets.

Nothing that ever happens isn't irreversible. I'm not the type of person that thinks that every break for someone else is a step back for you. My final advice, and it's what I've said to myself, is 'no more wankers'. Don't deal with them, learn to say no to them. Listen to your gut instinct.

 Key idea

One more time: don't underestimate your value.

·Next step

In the next chapter we look at how to get that elusive book deal.

10

Getting a book deal

This chapter is aimed at those of you (and I imagine that is the majority) who dream of having a book published. And by a 'book', I mostly mean a cookery book. Today cookery books are so covetable, so beautiful, it's the ambition of most cooks to have one published. I have literally hundreds of cookbooks, in every room of the house, including the toilet. I devour them, then devour the recipes. I hope this chapter will aid you on your path towards getting a cookbook published.

I've talked before about the importance of starting a blog. This will act as your portfolio. This is another reason to stay away from brand-led blogging; it will use up your energy and time but not give a lot back in return long-term. If you want to be a professional food writer, think about what publishers might want to see. It helps to have a niche.

 ## Key idea

A top tip from me: if you want to come to the attention of publishers, review food books on your blog. At least twice a year I will do a big round-up cookbook post, one before Christmas, say, in November, and another before the summer holidays. Christmas is when people buy food/cookbooks as gifts and summer holidays is when people have time to read. People tend not to take cookbooks on holiday, so for the summer holiday reading post, I will recommend paperbacks such as food fiction or food and travel books or barbecue/summer outdoor food cookbooks. Why is this a good tip? Because publishers read reviews, and once they read your blog they may become interested in the rest of your writing.

Why publish a book?

Remember that you don't earn much money from books. There is some debate regarding advances: is it better to have a big advance meaning it will take a while to start earning royalties (because you will have to pay off your advance first)? Or is it better to hold out for a decent royalty payment? Some authors say if a publisher doesn't give you a good advance, they have less interest in promoting the book.

But a book is valuable in many other ways. It enhances your reputation and means you can access a different and wider audience. There are less book signings nowadays (so often you end up on your own perhaps selling one or two books) but you may be invited to some literary festivals, which can be great fun. I went to the Isle of Wight literary festival and gave a talk in conjunction with Jack Monroe, the 'austerity blogger'. Over breakfast in the hotel, I met author Louis de Bernières, who told me his favourite recipe for cooking Brazilian *feijoada*. You don't get paid to attend literary festivals, but usually they will pay your hotel and travel plus you get to attend the event. De Bernières said to me: 'As an author, it can be a lonely life; this is my way of socializing, of meeting my readers and other authors.'

There are also food festivals that may invite you to do a demonstration or a talk. It's worth getting in touch with local food festivals, letting them know you live in their area.

There are larger food events such as the Cake and Bake Show held twice a year. So, for instance, for my afternoon tea and baking book, *MsMarmitelover's Secret Tea Party* (2014), I've been in touch with the Cake and Bake Show and will give a talk. This is the right audience for that particular book and I hope I will sell a few copies.

Usually the publisher will give you between 8 and 12 free books; after that, you have to negotiate with your publisher the price at which you can buy your own book. It is most likely 50 per cent of the retail price. When you do an event, this is an opportunity to make a little extra cash by selling the book, signed, at the retail price. (The odd book or two always goes missing at an event; it's as if the audience doesn't realize that you as the author have to pay for every copy. So do keep an eye out!)

Key idea

Is there any difference between writing about food and writing about any other subject? There is. You want people to use what you've written. There is a responsibility to the readers, unlike in other writing such as fiction. If you've written a recipe, and people have gone out and bought the ingredients, and set aside time to cook it, it has to work.

Awards

Do enter awards. Several of them now have an online writing/ blogging category. Winning awards is useful to your career. The main ones in the UK are:

- **The Guild of Food Writers awards.** The Guild runs yearly awards, one of which is best food blog, which I won in 2013. I got a book deal directly off the back of that win. You don't have to be a member to enter the awards. *Deadline:* January. *Shortlist:* April. *Award winners announced:* May/June. There's a big party with everyone important in the food world. Canapés and drinks can be patchy, depending on who is sponsoring it. *Tip:* they tend to like quite traditional cookery writing, with good photographs and well-tested recipes. www.gfw.co.uk

- **Fortnum & Mason awards.** This is a newish one, in its third year, but already highly respected, partly because there is no perceived bias. There are two online categories: food writing and restaurant reviewing. I won for food writing in 2014. You enter yourself with selected pieces. *Deadline:* 31 January. *Shortlist:* April. *Awards:* May. Elegant enjoyable party on the top floor of the Fortnum & Mason store in London's Piccadilly with lots of champagne and good canapés. www.fortnumandmasonawards.com

- *Observer Food Monthly* **awards.** This is a very prestigious award from perhaps the UK's premier newspaper food magazine supplement. *Deadline:* June. *Shortlist and winners announced:* immediately prior to the awards in October. Getting an invite to the awards party means that you are somebody. There are always good cocktails and food, often by top chefs. (Since you ask, yes, I have been invited on occasion.) *Tip:* for the blogging award, they tend to go for quite newsy/gimmicky online writers. They also like writers with an ethical/political stance. Previous winners include a child who wrote about school dinners and a homeless austerity food blogger. For the book awards, they tend to go for their own food writers, published in *The Guardian* and *The Observer*. www.theguardian.com/observer-food-monthly-awards

- **Young British Foodies.** These quite new awards have a less conventional approach that seeks to celebrate the innovative in food. There are awards for chefs and food producers and there is now also a food writing category. *Deadline:* Seems to change every year so check the website. *Shortlist and winners announced:* September. Groovy hipster party with cocktails and the latest trendy street food. www.the-ybfs.com

Awards exist to publicize the publications or bodies that award them. They will sometimes give you a 'badge' to put on your site.

There is a little bit of code in the badge that drives traffic to their site.

Getting an agent

Try to get an agent. You pay them 15 per cent (plus VAT) but they will get your foot in the door. But do sack them if they are useless. I'm on my fourth. I'd read in books and seen in movies that your agent is like your best friend, nursing you through books and problems, facilitating your 'gift'. Not had too much of that myself. My first one left because she was pregnant. My second one didn't seem to believe in me at all. My third one never replied to my emails – for six months. You can get by without an agent but you are going to need advice for the contract. Literary agents have boilerplate contracts and standard templates for book deals.

Another option is to find your own book deal and find a specialist publishing lawyer to do the contract. This will save you the 15 per cent plus VAT which you pay on your advance and on all your sales royalties on the book.

To be frank most of my book deals, bar one, I've got myself. Publishers have approached me directly. I still go through the agent, though. The role of an agent is also to mediate between yourself and the publisher, to make sure that, even if there are disagreements, that the nasty bits are dealt with by the agent and therefore you get to retain a good relationship. He/she can also renegotiate deadlines.

Key idea

You can find agents by going on to the Association of Authors' Agents website (agentsassoc.co.uk) or checking out the latest edition of the *Writers' & Artists' Yearbook*.

Book advances

Expect anything from £3,000 to £25,000 for a first book. It's only if you are in the Pippa Middleton stratosphere of celebrity that you can get more. Not all of us can get our sisters to marry the future king. Sometimes publishers appear to suffer from a bizarre collective hysteria and start a bidding war, driving up the advance. A recent example of this in the food world is the case of Tim Hayward, author of *DIY Food* (2013), who got a massive advance for a two-book deal, literally hundreds of thousands of pounds. Hayward is a brilliant food writer but this did seem to be an inordinate amount of money for someone who wasn't on TV. This led to a great deal of envy within the food writing industry, I can tell you, and in fact I would say it rather harmed his book chances at awards because everyone was so furiously jealous. *DIY Food* was a beautiful book but didn't particularly sell well. Hopefully, his second book, on baking (based on his Cambridge bakery and café), will do better. Baking is a more saleable concept than making your own sausages from scratch.

 Key idea

Make sure you register with ALCS and the PLR. This will provide extra dosh for you as an author. Every little bit helps!

The ALCS is the Authors' Licensing and Collecting Society, an organization that makes sure authors get paid when, say, organizations such as educational institutions or businesses or government departments photocopy sections of their book or use sections of their book. It is free to register. Make sure that you register all your books and any magazine or newspaper articles you have written. They have reciprocal agreements with other countries, so register any foreign editions as well.

PLR is the Public Lending Right. Whenever someone borrows your book in the UK or Ireland from a library, you get a small fee. Registration with PLR is free. It's also rather nice to see how many people got your book out of the library that year.

 Snapshot exercise: Research the market

Think about who your book will appeal to. Who will buy it? Why will it be popular? Are there any other books like it? Read the competition. Are you doing anything different/better?

You can include the results of your research in your book proposal (see Workshop below).

Sleepers

Some cookbooks become popular slowly. Like J.K. Rowling's first Harry Potter book, they may struggle to find a publisher, but through personal recommendation they become sleeper hits. It must be very satisfying for the authors, even more than if, say, they had a popular TV series and knew that their accompanying book would be a sure-fire tie-in success.

Yotam Ottolenghi and Sami Tamimi had difficulty finding a publisher when they did the rounds with their first book, *Ottolenghi: The Cookbook*. I think they got a very small advance, something like £2,000 (and this was just before the crash when publishing advances did a nosedive) and eventually it came out in 2008. The rest is history, *Ottolenghi* has become a modern classic, its success down to pure word of mouth, people recommending it to each other.

Much the same happened to *The Flavour Thesaurus* (2010) by Niki Segnit. The moment we knew this was an establishment favourite was when we spied it on the bookshelf in Prime Minister David Cameron's kitchen during a photo op at Number 10. This is a very unusual food book, not really a cookbook, in which the author has ingeniously made a compendium of flavour combinations and what goes with what, some of them very unusual. There are some recipes embedded within the text but mostly it's a kicking-off point for inspiration. Every cook should have this book.

Interview: Michael Alcock, founder of Johnson & Alcock literary agency

Michael has been working in publishing one way or another for most of his career. He studied Classics at university, then moved to Greece and Turkey, where, in his words, he learned to 'eat properly, good food, forget the white tablecloth!' He then became a sales rep for a publisher in northern Europe, so he was eating out a lot as he was away for long periods of time. Michael subsequently worked as an editor in various publishers, finally becoming the head of cookery for Pan Macmillan. He got the English-language rights of

> the top French chefs in the late 1970s and 1980s and published
> Caroline Conran. There was a new attitude to food developing at
> this time, moving on from the post-war austerity. It was an exciting
> time. He created the Johnson & Alcock literary agency in 2003, so
> he knows this business from the bottom up.

What should writers do to get a book deal?

If you want a book deal, research the competition: who is publishing
what and who bought similar books. Look on Amazon and online
book sites such as Waterstones but also go into bookshops and feel
the books, see the quality.

Your proposal should be better, complementary, different. The
people you really have to impress are the sales people. Editors can
be romantic. You are not just aiming to appeal to the commissioning
editor; he/she has to convince colleagues in sales, marketing,
production and finance. Think about whether five thousand people
would want to buy your book: that's the test. Research with the
public at cookery events.

Talk to people. You need to raise your profile: I would also suggest
that you have a blog or a supper club or try to get a column in a
local paper. Even if you aren't paid, it's exposure. Try to create a
community, fans that love your work so you have a ready-built
audience. Base your proposal on your research, develop a platform,
a brand, a cooking club, a USP. No one will notice it otherwise.

Do you recommend TV reality shows as a way to come to the attention of the public?

Reality-show winners and contestants do well. But it's a fake test. If
you are telegenic it can work. But with the *Bake-off*, baking is done
according to nationalities. Each nation likes to bake its own recipes.

What is your advice about getting an agent?

Agents look for things in the press so if your project has had some
press that is a positive thing. All the big agencies such as Curtis
Brown have a food section. There are ten great food publishers in
London. They are the ones with the resources. An agent will be
pitching your book, using who he has relationships with in the
publishing world. He will get your foot in the door. A lot of agents
don't reply to emails. At Johnson Alcott, all the mail goes into a pile

and an assistant will sort through the mail and divide up anything interesting among the agents. Publishers like Penguin only accept manuscripts through agents.

Choose an agent that deals with non-fiction, and make your proposal 20 to 30 pages maximum. Emailing is acceptable. Most agents are tech-friendly. And if you include some pictures, the backlight on the screen will make the food pictures stand out. But if you are not a techie, send a hard copy to the agent.

So how does a budding author come up with a new idea?

It's difficult to come up with something completely new as most cookery writers adapt the past. Seaweed cookery is a new thing as is sustainable cooking. Health-based cookery writing dealing say with IBS or food intolerances is popular. There is now every speciality of regional cooking: Puglian, Keralan, Sri Lankan. Think outside the food box.

Do you have any other tips?

The visual is important. It's not just the printed word. Most cookery books are bought as presents or as coffee-table books. Nowadays with blogs and apps, you can easily look up recipes.

One final thing: write in a plain legible font in black in at least 12 point. I've received emails from wannabe authors where the font is a) Comic Sans b) pink c) minute, like 8 point. You can't even be bothered to read these. It doesn't make you look like a character; it makes you look like a nutter, somebody who isn't serious.

The proposal

You need to write a proposal that your agent will send around to his/her publisher contacts. It's a bit like a CV for your book: you want to pull in the editor with tantalizing glimpses of your masterwork but not give all the secrets away. (You don't want them to think, 'Ooh that's a good idea, and I'll get my pet celebrity/ghostwriter combo to write it.' (Think I'm being cynical? This has happened.)

I'll spend a couple of weeks on a proposal. David Lebowitz, on the other hand, spent nine whole months writing a proposal. Apparently, this is common in the United States, plus they will get two or three years to write the book. Here it's anything from two to six months, rarely longer. And this writing time is getting shorter; cookbooks are becoming rushed affairs. I think this is a pity. I need time just to think about the book, cogitate, research, gear myself up into writing it. (So the sooner you start really thinking about it the better.)

When you're ready, use the following workshop to help you put your proposal together:

Workshop: Write a proposal

1 Try to sum up your book in 20 words. Then list five key points that make your book unique and marketable (see the Snapshot exercise above). Then, in half a page, summarize in a lively, informative and creative way the basic premise of your book.

2 Come up with a title and subtitle. Keep these short and make sure they grab attention.

3 Write a short biography about yourself including:
   - a bio of 50 words
   - a photo of yourself
   - your experience in the field that you are writing about, including supporting activities such as events, talks, qualifications, courses led, radio or TV appearances, awards, etc.
   - why you are the best person to write this book
   - your email, phone number and address
   - the links and stats of your blog/website, Twitter, YouTube, Pinterest, Instagram and so on, as applicable.

4 References and quotes: do you have contacts in the field, ideally celebrities or respected people, who would endorse your book?

5 Outline the contents with chapter headings and summaries. It is good to give as much detail as possible at this stage. Bullet points are good as is a complete list of recipes.

6 You also need to include a sample chapter. This should be about 5,000 words. If you are writing a cookbook, write at least ten sample recipes with introductions.

The publishing process

A book will take one to two years to be published. Normally, for a cookbook, you need six months to write it, and at least six months' post-production encompassing editing, photography, design, printing, launch and publicity.

Sometimes there is a choice of when to publish it. You don't want to publish from September to November because that is when all the big guns, the TV chefs, the known names, bring their cookbooks out for Christmas. Your 'little' book will get drowned in terms of publicity and in terms of display in bookshops. Spring is good. August isn't great but the end of August is good, just before the celebrity onslaught and after the summer when everyone is away.

Think whether the subject matter is conducive to the time of year: there is no point bringing out a barbecue book in the winter.

Unfortunately, publishers are also really, really slow. Everything takes forever to be decided. For my first book, *Supper Club* (2011), I met the editor (at a party!) in November 2009. By December 2009 she'd said yes to the proposal. I started the book in February 2010 with a July 2010 deadline. The photography took place in August 2010. The book came out in April 2011. What happened between August 2010 and April 2011 apart from printing the book (which took place in the Far East because it's cheaper), I don't know. At the time I felt that this was a very leisurely pace. In the world of online writing, you write it, you publish it – it's all very instantaneous. In fact, the slow pace really worried me. Interest in supper clubs as a phenomenon was waning by the month; the press had done it to death and were bored. In the end, the book came out too late to be really on trend for a trend that started beginning 2009 and too early for it to be a mass phenomenon. It also came out just before a royal wedding when nobody in the UK thinks about anything else but the royals. Plus that March/April happened to be one of those bizarre UK heat waves. Nobody buys cookbooks in a heat wave.

So all in all this was a rather unfortunate publishing date. But *Supper Club* is a beautifully produced book. It's one of those books that will sell slowly but steadily for years. So it didn't exactly burn its way up the charts but has continued to sell. I'm even getting royalty cheques

So back to the slowness of publishers. Letters sent by post rather than email are called 'snail mail'. Book publishing is the writing version of this, 'snail publishing'. Publishing is still a very old-fashioned industry, struggling to adapt to an online, Internet-based, free-content world. Bookshops are closing. Everything is being bought, heavily discounted, online, and many people are not buying paper or hardbacks but e-reader/tablet versions. However, the more beautifully produced your book, the more likely people are going to buy it in book form for their coffee tables or as a gift.

THE COOKBOOK PHENOMENON

Cookbooks are more expensive to produce. But cookbooks are 30 per cent of the publishing market and growing. In fact, someone like Jamie Oliver, who does print runs of 100,000, will in some way be financing all those little experimental authors that Penguin gives advances to, in the hope that they strike gold. Most cookbook authors have print runs of 5,000 to 20,000.

It's rare that you as a cookbook author are given money for ingredients. If you are a ghostwriter, however, you will be given an ingredient allowance.

Trust is important. Trust that recipes work. You absolutely must test recipes. Schedule-wise you may not have the luxury of testing each recipe several times on different ovens, in different kitchens. In the old days, the likes of Claudia Roden were paid by the *Sunday Times* to travel around Italy every month for a year in order to research her Italian food book. As a result her Italian food book is a classic of the genre and a work that does not date. She would have been testing extensively but gradually, incorporating the recipes into her family meals. Nowadays, unless you are independently wealthy, this kind of in-depth research is unlikely to occur.

Nonetheless, testing recipes is at the very core of a cookbook: you must test each recipe at least once. Sometimes you may adapt a standard recipe and shove that in, thinking that it is bound to work. You'd be surprised: even recipes on reliable sites like BBC Food sometimes do not work. I cannot emphasize the testing enough. If you haven't, you will get caught out by the queries editor. I worked with Anne Sheasby on *MsMarmitelover's Secret Tea Party* and while at first I resisted her meticulous work, in the end I grew to appreciate and learn from it.

Nothing was taken for granted. Look at the section on writing recipes in Chapter 5 to find out more.

Key idea

While on average only one recipe is cooked from a book (yes, that *is* a depressing statistic), you must make sure that every single recipe in your book does work. Do ask for help with testing. Once you've written the recipe, test it yourself and get others, family, friends, blog readers, members of your Facebook page, to retest it. You want a fresh head to test your recipe and feed back on what doesn't work.

THE PUBLISHING TEAM

- The **commissioning editor** is the person who agreed to the book deal, the commissioner. They will have overall control. Sometimes they are the managing editor as well.

- The **managing editor** takes care of the day-to-day process of bringing your book to publication, co-ordinating members of the team, keeping schedules and budgets.

- The **copyeditor** will firstly check your grammar and spelling. If you don't write very well, they will turn your work into proper sentences. They will juggle stuff about, point out repetitions and so on.

- The **recipe 'query' editor** is generally an experienced cook. They will ask you questions about your recipes. They will query quantities and methods. They will point out missing bits. This can take weeks.

- The **art director/designer** will oversee the general look of the book. They will choose fonts and a colour palette. They will normally design the cover. They will often attend the photo-shoots and keep a steady hand on the tiller, steering the visual team back to the look.

- The **photographer,** obviously, will photograph the book. They will usually have at least one assistant who will do the digital postproduction.

- The **home economist** will cook and style the food. They will often have an assistant, too. If you are shooting eight dishes a day, this is a copious amount of work and responsibility. This person will also double-check that the recipes work (though this is for a minority of recipes: the ones being photographed).
- The **props stylist** goes to the prop houses and chooses the props within the colour palette that the art director has selected. They will also hire tabletops and fabrics.

 Key idea

Ask questions. How many pages will there be in the book? How many recipes? How many will be photographed? Make sure you get some input on the shot list – you as the author know best which of your recipes look visually appetising.

HITCHES

Every book I've ever done I've been dissatisfied with and so has every author I've ever met. There are some pages I literally wince at. The ideal is to be in total control but publishing is collaborative. And remember the publisher is spending a great deal of money, so ultimately it's their decision. I've had disagreements over the cover of *MsMarmitelover's Secret Tea Party*, which I also photographed. I shot a cover that was a suggestion by the first editor. But the all-important decision makers are Sales. They're the people who have to go out and sell your book to bookstores and they get to veto design decisions. My first cover was quite elaborate and had fondant fancy cakes in the picture. 'Too difficult!' Sales pronounced. 'The amateur baker won't want to tackle that.' It was an interesting perspective that I hadn't considered.

So that cover, which I'd spent a week on, was rejected. So, under the aegis of Sales (imagine this being said with a hiss because, let's face it, no sales department is exactly known for its visionary artistic creativity), the publisher got an illustrator to do a pale-violet cover (when the colour palette of the inside was very much themed red and white) with a cut-out photo of one of my cakes. A friend said: 'Oh scrapbooking is all the rage, that's probably the look they are going for.' I contemplated asking for my name to be removed from the book if they published it with this cover. It was vile. At the time of writing, I still don't know what the cover will be. Fingers crossed. It might end up being called *MsNobody's Secret Tea Party*.

Postscript: we ended up with a strikingly cheerful red-and-white gingham cover, with bits of gold lettering. The sort of thing you can see from the back of the shop. That's important.

Snapshot exercise: Promoting the book

Do you have contacts that will publicize the book? Does the subject matter coincide with a holiday or festival or anniversary connected with the book? Do you have a large social media presence that can help promote the book?

Snapshot exercise: Sales

How many books could you see via your own mailing lists?

Are there any foreign markets that could be interested in the book?

Are there any organizations that may be interested in the book (associations/ corporations/museums/tourist centres/supermarkets)?

Other publishing options

If you can't get a book deal, all is not lost – do consider the other options.

E-PUBLISHING

Sometimes self-published books get taken up by mainstream publishers. The most famous example of this, of course, is E.L. James's *Fifty Shades of Grey* (2012), which started out as an ebook and a print-on-demand, but got picked up by Vintage, part of Random House. It became one of the best-selling books of all time.

In the food world the equivalent is the illustrated book *In at the Deep End* by Jake Tilson, which was written, designed, photographed, everything, by this artist. He did the entire book as an inkjet dummy and presented it to Quadrille who published it as it was. This book was nominated for the Guild of Food Writers book awards in 2012. Jake recommends perseverance and takes this approach because he 'wants to be in control of the whole book'.

INTERVIEW WITH VIVIEN AND NIGEL LLOYD

*Marmalade expert and jam maker Vivien Lloyd (*www. vivienlloyd.com*) and her husband, Nigel, have self-published a hardback book,* First Preserves (2011), *as well as several ebooks (*Marmalades, Jams, Chutneys *and* Fruit Curds*).*

Could you explain something about the different ways of selling ebooks?

Nigel: There are two ways of selling your self-published books: through Amazon, which owns Kindle, and through iBooks, which is owned by Apple. Both methods cost money and you have to weigh up which is better for your project.

Both methods take around 30 per cent of the cover price. But they are priced differently: Amazon charges 10p per megabyte. So if you have a large file because you have photographs or video, you may be better off going with iBooks which charges a straight 30 per cent.

Which is easier to use?

Vivien: Both Apple and Amazon offer free software for the book-designing process. The Apple software produces a better result, but is more complex and you may need a book/graphic designer. To produce Kindle books you need to convert your Word or Pages file into an ePub file and there is free software called Calibre, which helps you edit and adjust the formatting of the ePub file and is simple to use.

What are the advantages of self-publishing?

Vivien: It's a way for me to communicate my passion without depending on a big publishing house. I have control and can produce a high-quality book. We have produced much better ebooks than most large publishers.

Nigel: I went to a talk at the Cheltenham Literary Festival a year or so ago, where an experienced bookseller and a director of a major publisher were talking. The problem is the main publishing houses appear to have a conflict of interest: they don't really want to encourage ebooks. When they produce ebooks, generally they simply copy the hardback into an ebook and it rarely looks good. You have to work differently for ebooks.

Would you recommend doing a hardback or an ebook?

Vivien: Both, but a hardback is more expensive. Plus you have to store it. We did print runs of 2,000 books, which is a tonne, a square metre of books. At the moment they are under our daughter's bed.

With an ebook you can also do video, which is very useful for what Vivien does: teaching people how to make preserves.

What was the toughest hurdle?

Nigel: Setting up the accounts on Amazon and iBooks. It's fiddly and complicated. It took me a couple of days.

Writing, photographing, designing the books is enjoyable and easy but marketing and distributing the books is difficult.

You need a certain amount of money to invest in the first place. We spent £10,000 on the book and another £10,000 on the website and publicity.

It cost £4,000 for each print run of 2,000 books. Another £6,000 for the photography, design and other ancillary costs. So far we've recouped around £8,000.

If doing a self-published hardback, how do you sell it apart from on Amazon?

There are two methods: your own website, marketed through social media, or physical shops. You can go to Waterstones which has a community service in which they sell books by local authors. It buys the books from you, not sale or return, and are reasonable payers, paying the invoice within three months.

We've given up supplying independent bookshops, however, because getting paid is problematic and time-consuming.

If selling online what advice do you have?

Nigel: Set up author pages on Amazon. Vivien has these pages on Amazon.com and Amazon.co.uk plus the French and German sites.

Her Twitter feed is there and we can upload videos. (Videos really help sell books on Amazon).

The title of the book is fiercely important. The first word of the title is what you want to plug. For instance, if you search 'marmalade' on Amazon.co.uk/books, her marmalade book is on page 3. (The first title is by Sarah Randall, published by a mainstream publisher. They get precedence in the Amazon charts.)

If you search 'jam' and 'chutney', Vivien is nowhere to be found. There are too many mainstream books about jam. However, if you search 'fruit curds', Vivien's book is number one.

It's also worth thinking about other markets: Vivien's books sell well in Australia while the United States is very interested in fruit curd. It's worth thinking about using 'US-friendly' terms like 'jelly' for jam.

Marmalade is more popular in certain countries and is seasonal. Events like the *Paddington* movie also increase interest in marmalade.

Another thing to consider is VAT and tax.

This year the EU has just changed the law on ebooks. Before, you paid 3-per-cent VAT because it was ostensibly sold from Luxembourg. Now the law has changed and VAT is based on the purchaser's country so in the UK the VAT is 20 per cent and in Ireland it is 23 per cent.

What are the cons of self-publishing?

Nigel and Vivien: You don't make any money! Illustrated books, either hardback or ebook, are difficult to make a profit from, as they are expensive to produce. Many people still have black-and-white Kindles so they won't be interested in a cookbook. The things that do very well as ebooks are self-help books or fiction; text-based books.

Nigel Lloyd is available for consultation and help on self-publishing. Contact him at Nigel@vivienlloyd.com

---

CROWDFUNDING

Crowdfunding is another option. Niamh Shields of Eatlikeagirl.com crowdfunded her book about bacon, raising a whopping £24,000.

Granted, Niamh has a large fan base, writing one of the longest-running food blogs in the UK. She's hired her own photographer and designer and will get the book printed up herself. The only real problem doing it this way is storage and distribution. Do you really want a home full of thousands of books?

Check out Lulu (www.lulu.com) for small runs. Unbound (unbound.co.uk), the brainchild of John Mitchinson, also takes on authors who have great ideas but are having difficulty finding a publisher. Some of their authors are quite famous.

Unbound will help you do the crowdfunding. You make a video pitch on their site and with any luck supporters will get behind your idea and make pledges of money. I bought one book this way, made by a graphic designer friend of mine. It was more expensive than usual, because obviously there is no economy of scale, but I wanted to support my friend and, most importantly, was interested to see a book on a subject that intrigued me, 1980s nightclub life. There wasn't a big enough audience for it to get a mainstream book deal, but it did have a small interested audience.

Writing a cookbook

You've got the commission, now you have to write the book. (Hollow laughter.) Try not to write completely in a vacuum. Just as you need a blogging buddy, you need a sounding board for your book – just someone to talk to. Every writer has a different technique. Some are super efficient and get up at 6 a.m. each day, whack out a couple of thousand words in a couple of hours, then have the rest of the day off.

If you are by nature a procrastinator who inhales entire series on Netflix in an attempt to avoid writing, you've got to make yourself work. Get up early, make some coffee, sit down and force yourself through the pain and procrastination barrier. Just write it down, word by word.

Sometimes it flows. Oh those days are good!

Catherine Phipps, author of *The Pressure Cooker Book* (Ebury Press, 2012) and *Chicken: Over 200 Recipes Devoted to One Glorious Bird* (Ebury Press 2015) remarks:

'There are days when I'm clear headed and nothing gets in my way. I'll sit down early in the morning and write solidly all day, maybe 12,000 words. I'll only get up to go to the toilet. And I edit at the same time, so that 12,000 words will end up as 5,000 or 6,000 words. That's a good day, and I'll have one of those every couple of weeks.'

Catherine Phipps's technique for writing a book is quite random. She'll look at her recipe list and pick something and start work on it. She often writes the preparatory work in long hand, using sticky notes. She'll flip from one thing to the next. She'll make bullet points.

I use Scrivener, a useful bit of software for structuring a book. Writing is a lot easier if you know what you want to say. Catherine uses Word and creates a new document for each chapter. She puts the recipe list pertaining to that chapter at the top of each chapter. A lot of that gets thrown out. She uses hers as guidance. She often refers back to her proposal – there may be some ideas in there that she has forgotten about. The list of recipes will keep evolving. She will write an outline introduction at the top of each chapter. Below she will add recipes, stringing them together, though each recipe will have a little introduction. The recipe introduction will be about an ingredient or a method or an anecdote. At the end of each chapter, she will return to the chapter introduction and write and edit it to reflect the content of the chapter.

 ## Key idea

If you are using Word, don't delete your notes, just use the strike-through function. This way you aren't throwing everything out. Obviously, at the end, before you hand your typescript in, you will need to delete any extraneous material.

Ghostwriting

An option you may not have considered is ghostwriting but if you are an efficient recipe writer then do not dismiss this: ghostwriters can earn more than authors. On your own name your advance may be £3,000 to £10,000. However, if you are writing under the name of a famous author, you can earn double that, around £18,000 to £20,000. It takes a certain kind of personality to ghostwrite, however. You must almost 'channel' the personality of the person you are ghosting. You have to possess a very small ego. You must be prepared for someone else to get all the credit for your hard work. You will see the chef going on TV doing interviews talking about how he/she wrote the book and know it was you that sweated over every word, every recipe. Make no mistake: virtually every TV chef has a ghostwriter. Notable exceptions are Nigella Lawson and Nigel Slater, but they will obviously have a team who shop and test for them.

To spot the ghostwriter, check the back of the book where authors give thanks for all the help. Sometimes the ghostwriter is called the 'editor'; other times they are just a mystery name who is given thanks. The ghostwriter must keep it a secret – this is usually in the contract. Some chefs are generous with the credit: Heston Blumenthal insisted, for instance, that the Guild of Food Writers made another award for the ghostwriter of one of his award-winning cookbooks.

Next step

You've got the book deal, now get on TV… or radio!

11

Getting on TV and radio and how to make a cookery video

I realize this book is, strictly speaking, about food writing but, even so, you've got to sell it. The best and quickest route to publicizing your work is on TV or radio. There's no point being a writer of genius if nobody gets to hear of your stuff.

Radio

Don't underestimate the importance of radio in building your food brand. Listen to food radio programmes such as Radio 4's *The Food Programme* and the same station's food quiz show, *The Kitchen Cabinet*, and you will get a feel for the medium's possibilities.

Food writer Vanessa Kimbell took a very clever approach to becoming known in the world of food. She got a regular Sunday spot with Radio Northamptonshire as part of someone else's show. Every week she would invite somebody notable in the food world, for instance *Waitrose Magazine* editor William Sitwell, to be on the show, thereby creating good content for the programme and making a good contact. She then started a blog on how to write a cookbook, involving her readership in the process. Vanessa eventually got to do the odd spot on Radio 4's *The Food Programme* and is now writing her second cookbook.

INTERVIEW WITH SHEILA DILLON

Sheila Dillon is a food journalist, specializing in the politics of food, and the presenter of BBC Radio 4's The Food Programme. *She has won multiple awards for her investigative work into food, including the Glaxo Science Prize, the Caroline Walker Award and several Glenfiddich Awards, as well as awards with* The Food Programme *team at the Guild of Food Writers and the Fortnum & Mason food awards.*

How did you get into radio? Why food?

I got experience in food journalism while living in New York. In New York I wrote for a magazine called *Food Monitor* which had articles about development and links with health. At the time, Ronald Reagan was breaking the meat industry unions and this was a good story. First I volunteered for *Food Monitor* and also for a community feeding programme in The Bronx. Then I was offered a job on the magazine. I wrote a column called 'Foodbiz'.

When I was living in New York there was a pesticide scandal on Long Island, which is a huge potato-growing area. Pesticides had leached into the aquifer, and had poisoned wells. I was feeding my baby at the time, often mashed-up potatoes, and I wondered how much of this pesticide was in the potatoes. This was pre-Google so

I went to the library and looked up information about safe levels of pesticide. I discovered that pesticide levels were only tested on adult males and it was calculated that an average male ate four potatoes a week. Nobody was writing about this, so I thought: Why don't I?

When I returned to the UK, I looked through the *Radio Times* and contacted the producer of *The Food Programme*. I had no experience in radio. I pitched some ideas. But remember these were rich times, the late 1980s. There was money. In those days it wasn't so competitive in the world of food and the area I specialized in, the politics of food, hardly anybody was doing.

The ideas I pitched to *The Food Programme* were based on some of these issues particularly organic food production, which was just emerging. In those days the BBC trained people whom it felt had potential: I was sent on a week's production course by the BBC. This no longer exists for freelancers.

Why food?

I've always cooked and loved food. I had worked on Wall Street as a cook for a commodities broker and helped out a friend's catering company.

Plus, I'm dead greedy! But I was a journalist as well as a cook, always political, always feminist. But it never occurred to me that I could be a journalist about food.

What advice do you have for people wanting to do food radio? Is there training?

Nowadays there are private training courses. But if someone has a good pitch, we might run it. We'll lend them equipment. It's not a commission, but we'll pay if it's used.

For instance, David Baker, who was a managing editor of *Wired*, has just done a food story for us in Brazil where they have revitalized sugar production. He worked with one of our producers, Emma Weatherill, who sat down with him and worked on what he should bring back. Due to lack of budget we can't send people out to Brazil, so this was an opportunity for us to do a story on that part of the world which we normally wouldn't get to cover.

What advice do you have for people doing pitches and, if successful, recording?

Be persistent. I'm always amazed at how *un-persistent* people are.

Write two good paragraphs when pitching. Again, people don't do that.

Follow up.

Don't give up.

Honestly, the number of people who have pushed their good ideas and given up… Send a polite email.

We especially want women's voices.

Make sure that there is enough atmosphere, local sounds etc., in the recording. [Author's note: I was visiting Israel with some of the world's top food bloggers and was asked to record my visit by Radio 4. I was so busy concentrating on the food blogger story that I did not understand that they also wanted sounds of Israel. Because I missed out on that recorded atmosphere, the piece was never run. So learn from my mistakes!]

Please don't take rejection or ignored emails personally; it's rarely personal. Producers are incredibly busy, things slip, there's no budget. Take your courage in both hands and be a bit pushy.

There isn't much food radio, is there?

I think commissioning editors have woken up. They are keen on commissioning food programmes. It's always been a problem – editors thought of food as trivial, not serious, just as entertainment.

But that is changing: food journalist Andrew Webb just did an hour's food programming on Radio 4. I'm doing a 15-part series, each part 15 minutes long, which is about to be broadcast. On BBC Radio 3, there is no food. It's mostly classical music but has some speech/ideas programming. There is a new series starting on the World Service, called *The Food Chain*, using a network of correspondents.

I see no reason why the explosion of interest in food should not be reflected on radio. Radio is loved. People listen to it such a lot as they move about. And, of course, radio is something you can cook to…

What is the future of food radio? Are there any general trends?

Look online. There is a huge audience for online radio, a very young audience.

Look at Soho Radio, an online station in London that has a regular magazine-style food programme hosted by William Sitwell, former editor of *Waitrose Food* magazine.

There are more in the States (for instance: Heritage Radio Network which runs out of Robertas restaurant in Williamsburg, Brooklyn, New York). There are lots of gaps in the UK market in terms of food radio.

Given how popular online radio and podcasting is, there still isn't that much food radio.

In terms of the future, I think there needs to be the radio equivalent of *Sorted* and food vloggers. It needs to be rougher, more authentic. At the moment the BBC insists that any video on the Radio 4 website is perfect, although I'd prefer it to be more 'in the moment'.

Food is an international subject. You can reach out beyond your borders; you can communicate with everybody.

At its best food radio can be really inspiring.

Write exercise: Create a podcast

Write an outline on the local food in your area. Develop this into a three-minute script for a radio piece, taking into account the fact that people cannot see what is going on. Record it on your phone, if you can.

TV

To be on mainstream terrestrial TV, get an agent. This is hard, much harder, than getting a literary agent. TV agents will pick you based on who they have on their books already. They don't want someone in the same casting bracket. For instance, when I was searching for an agent, I found that 'nobody white and over 30' to be the remit of one top food TV agent. So don't take it personally if you aren't chosen, you may just not be the right type.

And remember fashions change. TV is very superficial, and it's getting worse. Cooks now need to look like models, especially if you are a woman. The days of *Two Fat Ladies* (a 1990s TV programme featuring two elderly overweight female cooks on a motorbike and sidecar) seem to be gone. They may come back, but right now it's all about female cooks who don't look as if they eat.

If you don't have the classic profile of the good-looking, youthful TV chef, do your best with what you've got. You never know: the pendulum may swing back to expertise and character. I suggest the following:

- Create a signature look – for example Gizzi's beehive.
- Get your teeth bleached. The single most ageing, impoverished 'look' is bad teeth. Spend money on them. This doesn't turn you into the Osmonds, but it does make you look great and feel more confident.
- Get your hair done, especially before a piece to camera, a photo session, or an important interview with someone influential. Nowadays TV people won't fork out for it. So pay for it yourself. It really is worth it.
- I'm going to assume, seeing as you are a food lover, that you may not be the most svelte person, figure-wise. In which case, all I can say is buy a strong set of 'Spanx' or a girdle. Even if you are a man.

DIY TV

Don't despair if you can't get on mainstream TV. The Internet has arrived! Start making your own.

One of the biggest traffic attractors is videos on your blog: use YouTube or Vimeo. Building a portfolio of work, a show reel, is also one of the aims of having your own YouTube channel.

YOUTUBE

YouTube has been instrumental in building up an alternative broadcasting medium, particularly with the younger demographic. In 2014 suddenly everybody became aware that there was this whole hidden tranche of emerging YouTube stars when Zoella, a YouTube beauty vlogger, was asked to be in the video for the Live Aid single. She wasn't a musician, but she is extremely influential, with literally millions of subscribers on her YouTube channel. It's only a matter of time before food vloggers have the same reach.

There's reason to get a YouTube channel going: when producers are casting for a show, they will often check YouTube.

Someone might make a suggestion and it takes only minutes to check out what they are like on YouTube – it will be an instant yes or no. So do make sure that your YouTube work is all of a certain quality where you are at your best.

VIMEO

Vimeo is another video service. Many video professionals use this. Unlike YouTube, you may have to pay to use this service, depending on your usage. There are three tiers, from basic, which is free, to $199 a year, if you are using it for business. It doesn't have as many viewers as YouTube – 100 million monthly as opposed to a billion – but you can post longer videos than on YouTube where you are restricted to just 15 minutes. Vimeo is of higher quality than YouTube. Another advantage of Vimeo is that there is less competition, and also it doesn't show 'videos like yours' at the end where people will click away from your channel.

You can also shoot short sections of video on Instagram, Vine and Twitter.

How to create a cookery video: a few pointers

ESSENTIAL EQUIPMENT

- **Camera.** Don't forget you can get great results from a smartphone. My iPhone 6 has ordinary video, slo-mo and time-lapse effects, all of which are incredibly easy to use. You can also use a laptop or an iPad. But if you want to invest a bit more, most cameras now have a video facility. At the high end, the Canon 5d does broadcast quality. You might also consider investing in a GoPro video camera, originally developed for sports enthusiasts, which can fix on to your head. This way you can film yourself, hands-free, cooking something. An entry level GoPro is around £100.

- **Tripod.** This could be a large portable travel tripod, useful for a larger video camera, or for lights, a tiny table-top tripod or even a curly one that you can wrap around something. Use a mobile phone holder if you are shooting on an iPhone.

LIGHTING

For longer set-ups you want a key light and a fill light. The quick option: a Rotolight (currently around £70) with gels (useful for adapting to different colour temperature lights; see Chapter 8 for more information). I've got one of these and it's very light to carry or pop in your handbag.

SOUND

Don't underestimate the importance of sound. In fact, to produce a more professional video, sound is more important than the visuals. You can tie together the look with a consistent audio track. If you like shooting videos, I would suggest that you invest a little money in buying a separate microphone so that the sound is not relying on the inbuilt camera mic. Rode do good products in this area.

You can buy a lapel microphone, which allows you to go into noisier areas and still hear what you are saying (this currently costs around £35). This will have a cord and you can thread the cord up your dress or shirt and wear it discreetly on your lapel. This will plug into your iPhone, iPad or stills camera with a video function; it also fits Android phones.

Consider also buying a mini boom mike (around £99) for general sound if you are in a quiet place.

Few people speak without 'ums', 'ahs', hesitations and breaths. This can be edited out of the audio track.

You can check recording quality on YouTube.

BASIC CAMERA SHOTS

Vary your shots – this will make the editing easier. Don't stay in the same place.

- **The establishing shot.** This is taken from a distance, giving a general view of the scene. If it's at a place, start outside and film where you are going to shoot. If it's a cooking video, start with a view of the kitchen. You will need a wide-angle lens for this and probably a tripod.

- **Wide shot.** This sets the context.
- **Close-up.** This could be on the face of the person talking, on details of the scene such as ingredients, or actions with the hands, say chopping. You need to zoom in or use a telephoto/long lens for this shot.
- **Pan shot.** Pan the camera around the scene. You can move the camera around slowly on the tripod.
- **Handheld shot.** This can add immediacy and fluidity to your video, but use the stabilizer on your camera so that your audience doesn't feel sick and dizzy.

Key idea

Keep it landscape: if shooting on a phone, remember to hold the phone horizontally. However, there is software and apps that will right things if you make a mistake. iMovie, for instance, can rotate images.

LENGTH

Keep it short. You need to tell the story in 90 seconds to a maximum of three minutes. Three minutes is a lot of screen time. How many times have you stopped watching a YouTube video because it took too long and you got bored?

In YouTube, in Settings, there are visual analytics and you can actually see when people are getting bored by when they click off.

Key idea

Think of your video as a pop single: short, sweet and catchy.

An interview should last about 30 seconds.

A tutorial would be longer, but you can speed up parts of it or use a time lapse. If a tutorial is very long, I suggest you split it into three-minute sections, clearly titled Parts 1, 2 and 3.

EXTRAS

You can also put in stills for artistic effect or at the introduction or conclusion stage. You can add text instructions for the recipes and a text recap at the end (especially if it's a recipe).

Snapshot exercise

Research the competition. What works?

For example, I really like the cooking videos by DulceDelight (Raiza Costa), a Brazilian blogger who lives in the United States. Her videos are short, brightly coloured and quirky. Her set is of a beautiful retro kitchen, and she selects great props both in the background and for cooking.

TIMING AND STRUCTURE

Start early: making a video takes longer than you think. Real cooking and cooking for the camera are different. You might have to do a 'Here's one I made earlier'.

Structure the 'show' logically. First do the introduction, then show the ingredients, do the preparation, cook, season, add any garnish or extra ingredients, then plate it up. The final shot should show a beautifully styled plate with a final wrap-up. Do a recap with the recipe in text and a link to your blog.

If you have someone else filming it, explain the cooking steps to them – crucial techniques must be captured in close-up.

Key idea

Remember, a cooking video is not only instructive but must also be entertaining.

STORYTELLING

Plan out your video, and keep in mind that you are telling a story. You can even make a storyboard, like a rough cartoon and a script. Most scripts and novels have three parts, so think of your 'story' in those terms.

SPEAKING TO THE CAMERA

To be comfortable speaking directly to the camera requires practice. You can look at the cameraperson if you wish. Once you are used to a crew, a cameraperson or filming by yourself, it's remarkably easy to talk to a camera lens. Just imagine that it is your audience. Try not to be self-conscious, though being relaxed comes with practice. Your cameraperson can have prompts written on cards, but don't attempt to read while talking – it looks/sounds bad.

WHICH RECIPE TO CHOOSE?

Try to pick a dish that can be prepped and cooked in less than an hour – at least until you become more experienced. That will result in, say, 30 minutes of footage, which will be edited down to three minutes. So remember that most of what you do will be edited out. I've found this to be the hardest bit: to compress all you want to say into a few sentences. That's why you need a script. Memorize this. (This is very hard. I had to do this while presenting a segment for BBC2's *Food and Drink* while trying not to look like a deer trapped in the headlights. This is why Jamie Oliver is a genius. He manages to make it all look so easy – the terribly difficult task of 'being yourself on camera'.)

> ## Key idea
>
> Have a script. If you don't, you will forget steps. Write down the ingredients and put it out of sight of the camera.

Never make a dish for the first time during your cooking video, pick tried-and-tested recipes. In terms of choosing your subject matter, think about what recipes haven't been filmed yet. This way your recipe video will not have too much competition in search results.

PREPARATION

Prepare all your ingredients and tools beforehand. Make a list of what you will need. Measure out ingredients into bowls, then you can just announce what is in them, for example '200g of plain flour', while the camera pans over the bowl of flour. The natural thing is to point at the bowls but this can mess with the continuity.

Make sure all of your equipment works. Give it a trial run.

LOCATION

Decide upon a shoot location. For most cooking recipes it is usual to shoot in the kitchen. If you are cooking hot food you need to be near an oven/stove/hob, which poses a problem as you will have your back to the camera and have to keep wrenching your head around. I'm always envious of people who have an 'island' in their kitchens, especially if the hob is installed on the 'island', as this means that they can face the camera naturally. If you aren't 'cooking' (i.e. using a hob or oven), then you can set up the shot anywhere in the house (although it would be rather surreal to be making salad in your bedroom). The point is: you can fake it. Shoot where the light is best. You can shoot most of the video on a corner of a table, say, next to a window and just use the kitchen 'set' when the oven is needed.

I did an outdoor cooking video in which we set up a two-burner camping stove in front of a background of zoo animals at a theme park because the theme was working with South African fruit. We set up a table facing the camera, with the stove, and I laid out all the ingredients in bowls. I used all retro enamel camping gear to display the food on, to go with the theme.

'Art direct' the set, arrange your shelves, and make sure that the space is tidy. Have a look in your camera to see how the background appears.

Shoot during the day. I've seen YouTube videos where people are shooting at night in their brown kitchens. The lighting is yellowy because it's shot with the light bulbs on overhead. The whole thing looks grim and dowdy. If you are working during the day, then shoot at the weekend. If your kitchen doesn't have great natural daylight, then fill in the daylight with a small light.

ANGLES

Normally, the camera should be level with your face or if, like me, you are a bit older, make sure that it's slightly above in order to avoid 'double chinitus'.

If using a laptop to film, put books underneath so it's not looking up at you.

Use a low angle/fork angle when pouring something.

If you have a cameraperson, then they could perch on a stool or ladder in order to shoot down on you while you are cooking or chopping.

If filming alone, you will have to put the camera on a tripod, take an establishing shot of you in your kitchen, and then a medium shot... close enough to see your face when talking but also with a wide enough angle to see your hands and cooking utensils/pots while cooking. You will have to 'cheat' with the close-ups later. For instance: if you want to film yourself cracking eggs into a bowl, set up the bowl, go to your camera and focus on the bowl and the side where your hands will be handling the eggs. Press the record button, scuttle around and crack the eggs, then go back to the camera to press pause.

It's definitely more tiring and time consuming doing it by yourself so, if you can get someone to help, do.

Key idea

Remember to shoot everything. Shoot at least ten seconds of everything, of each shot. Don't worry if you make mistakes, keep rolling the camera – these can be edited out.

VIDEO TITLES

Do keep your video titles very simple and very searchable, using the omnipotent 'keywords': so if it's a recipe for sesame-crusted seared tuna, put 'seared tuna steak'. Also, use the word 'recipe' in your title. 'Recipe' is one of the most searched words on the Internet.

WHITE BALANCE

This is the colour temperature (we talked about this a bit in Chapter 8). With video or film you want a good colour balance and many of the same lighting rules for photography also work for film. Most video cameras will have a white balance button. Use a white sheet of paper to focus on and adjust the white balance until it shows the white as a balanced white without blue or yellow or pink hues.

WHAT TO WEAR

Don't wear white or strongly patterned clothes. Solid, bright colours are best. I'm not saying dress like a newsreader, but those people wear those clothes for a reason – they look good on TV. Try to reinforce your brand's image through your look. Make sure that your clothing fits properly, too. Think about the length of your sleeves if you are prepping and cooking food. If you are wearing an apron, make sure that it's clean. Personally, I like hair tied back or at least not hanging in the food. I've seen arty Vimeos where good-looking girls who are supposed to be cooking are running their hands through their hair. Yuck. I don't care how beautiful and camera-ready you are, I don't want your hands in your hair then handling food.

Be aware that the camera puts on ten pounds or just over half a stone. Try not to get too depressed/hung up on this when you watch yourself. You'll get used to the way you look on camera.

If you are filming in a busy cluttered kitchen, think about what clothes will stand out and not clash with the colour scheme.

If you are wearing a lapel mike, then don't wear a necklace that you are tempted to fiddle with. You don't want a repeat of the famous necklace-clanging scene in *Singin' in the Rain*. If you are cooking, you might want to remove rings and bracelets, especially any cloth/rope friendship bracelets, which will look grubby and trail in the food – unless that's your brand, of course.

And make sure your teeth are looking good. I've mentioned teeth before but, if you are going to spend money on your appearance, forget the lipo or the nip and tuck and spend it on your teeth. Also think about what colours of clothes and make-up make your teeth look whiter. I have yellowish skin, so a bluish-hued red or pink lipstick looks good on me and makes my teeth look whiter. A yellowy shade makes my teeth look yellower. Do wear make-up (if you're a woman) and brush your hair. You'll need foundation because one can often look bleached out in lighting. If the lights are hot, you may need powder, too. Make sure that your lipstick and eye make-up are well applied and won't run, streak or smudge under hot lights.

TASTING FOOD ON CAMERA

Once I was cooking something in a big pot while being filmed for the BBC. The director kept asking me to taste the food, which I did.

Later, watching the film on the TV, while simultaneously tweeting about it, someone on Twitter said, 'Yuck, you are tasting from a big spoon then putting it back in the pot.' I run a home restaurant, so this is not a good reaction from a potential customer. So do think about what you do on camera.

In reality, most cooks have a mug of clean teaspoons from which to taste but, in the old days, chefs kept a spoon in their back pocket. Out it came into the dish, into the chef's mouth, then back into the pocket. Have you ever seen a chef on the pass of a high-end restaurant? They taste from each dish and don't have time to change spoon. Look, your mother tasted all your food, probably reusing the same spoon, and you didn't die. It's no big deal. A good kitchen is a place where all the food is being constantly tasted. Unless it's an open kitchen, you just won't know. Just don't do it on camera.

MAKING THE FOOD LOOK DELICIOUS

Always season from a height, it ensures the seasoning is evenly distributed and looks like a magic trick. Ta-da! Jamie Oliver is big on this. Use tricks like sieving icing sugar or flour from above. Use green garnishes to freshen up the plate. Drizzle your oil or cream slowly over the dish. Film the steam rising from the pot. Think of sounds like spitting oil as you fry. This is great close-up material for your food video. You want 'food porn' in your video. Stop and think before you eat everything and clear up. Have you got those shots?

THE FINAL SHOT: PLATING UP

Before shooting, choose the plate and props that you are going to display your finished dish on. If it's a cake, have a cake stand ready and a knife or cake slice for cutting, for instance. If the crew enjoy eating what you've made, film that, too.

EDITING

As I said before, your footage is going to be edited down to about three minutes. Lay the clips in sequential order in your editing software. Make sure that you have told the entire story from beginning to end. Then start to cut away material that is unnecessary. Use different 'cuts': jump cuts, J cuts and L cuts, fades and camera shots that go from blurs to focusing on one thing. You can also use split-screen techniques.

The simplest way to shoot a cooking video is to shoot it all in one take, zooming in for close-ups. You can then edit out all the extraneous ugly footage. The audio track will make it all fit together. It appears visually smooth.

You can slow down (or speed up) the visual – fractionally, perhaps 85 per cent of the speed, if you need it to fit with the sound.

There is lots of cloud-based editing software for iPhones. iMovie for the iPhone is very easy to use. You can also edit directly on YouTube.

For more complex shooting use iMovie on a Mac. Professionals will use Avid software. On a PC there is Final Cut Pro or Adobe Premiere. Most computers come with some sort of basic movie-editing software.

ADDING TEXT OR VOICEOVER

This is what ties it all together. The text will give added visual instruction, a place where people can pause and take notes. The voiceover can provide extra information and continuity. You can be creative with the text using interesting fonts or cursive, old-fashioned writing.

MUSIC

Music can add both fun and atmosphere to your video. Music enables you to spell out the mood of the piece. Use music as an introduction and finish as well as during passages where no words are needed. If you have a particular musical taste, this can also be a part of your brand.

You'd be surprised how dull most major movies would be without the thematic and atmospheric use of music. You don't have to use a voice track; you can use an instrumental if you like. If you make your own music, use that! With theme music there are two paths to take: either go along with the subject matter or use the music as a counterpoint to the visual action.

For instance, if you are demonstrating a French recipe, you could use French music. But rather than the traditional Piaf, Aznavour or Brel, try something more modern or *les années yéyé* (the French 60s). The music adds another whole layer of creativity.

Uploading video

When I've used video on my blog I've first uploaded it to YouTube then embedded it into my blog. It can take up to 24 hours for a video on YouTube to be uploaded but usually it takes around an hour. YouTube recommends MP4 but it will work with most formats. To get the best quality, try not to compress the video too much. iPhone footage is compressed and so it looks very grainy.

Below is some technical terminology that is useful to know:

- MP4 (a multimedia container format standard, specified as a part of MPEG-4)
- FLV (Flash Video, a kind of video format)
- AVI (Audio Video Interleaved, a kind of video format)
- MOV (the QuickTime multimedia file format)
- WMV (Windows Media Video)
- SWF (Shockwave Flash).

So that you don't get an effect called 'letter boxing' (which you will see on old panorama films), use an aspect ratio of 16:9 or 4:3.

The frame rate is usually between 25 and 30 frames per second. This fast rate is why video doesn't look as natural as film, which is slightly slower at 24 frames per second. *The Hobbit* trilogy was shot at 48 frames per second, which is why it looks strange to many.

HOW TO USE YOUTUBE

In 2015 YouTube is ten years old. So young! But it has changed how we watch media. It has created its own stars. Nowadays YouTube viewings contribute to the music charts: this has simply become the way that many people listen to music. Some YouTube videos get millions of views, more than standard TV stations. Jamie Oliver has started Food Tube, creating his own channel on YouTube and discovering a new generation of cookery stars that perhaps TV wouldn't have noticed. Food Tube is a low-risk way of creating new food content. When I want to know how to make a difficult recipe, perhaps something that I haven't entirely understood from the written instructions, I will search for it on YouTube. Sometimes seeing something being made is the only way to learn and now we can do that from the comfort of our own kitchens. We can teach ourselves to cook from YouTube videos.

YouTube is a free service: you don't have to pay anything to use it. In fact, you can earn money from it. Google bought YouTube and will prefer to push YouTube videos (as well as Google Hangout videos) rather than other platforms. If you want to include a YouTube video in your blog, use the 'embed' code on the YouTube video page and copy and paste it into the HTML section on the body of your blog.

 Key idea

> Blogs that embed video content get far more views. So this is a great way to get yourself, your blog and therefore your food writing noticed.

Keep your video to a maximum of ten minutes (though YouTube allows up to 15 minutes). 'Watch time' drives discovery rather than clicks. Watch time is the amount of time people spend watching your videos. So, for instance, if your video is boring and people click off, YouTube now take account of that in terms of ranking and recommendations. A lengthy 'watch time' improves the ranking of your video.

HOW TO GET DISCOVERED ON YOUTUBE

'Discovery' is the euphemism they use on YouTube meaning that people can find you. Because that's the whole point, isn't it? No point making a video if hardly anyone watches it.

YouTube analytics can help you know how well you're doing. Lots of comments help boost your profile. YouTube also does something called 'sentiment analysis' – whether the comments are positive or negative. The 'audience retention' report will tell you if the length of your videos is good or could be longer.

There are ways to attract views and subscribers: just as in blogging there is 'SEO', search engine optimization, in video there is VSEO, video search engine optimization.

You need good tags/keywords that are appropriate to your brand.

Your videos need good succinct titles, with good thumbnails that accurately describe the content. Think about scale. Think what would have impact when there is just a small image. They must be visually pleasing, but accurate about the content of the video and not misleading. Otherwise it can actively harm your reputation on YouTube.

Make a channel trailer to attract subscribers (people who are signed up to your channel). This trailer should be between 30 seconds and a minute. It should show why you are here, what you are about and how often they can expect new videos. The first 15 seconds are particularly crucial. That's the moment when people stay on or click off. Leave room at the end for a call to action: 'Please hit the subscribe button.'

The three lines in your channel description (the text above the fold) are all important as that is what is visible on your channel profile without the user having to click for more information. So get your key message in those first three lines. Use link shorteners such as Google or Bitly. Use appropriate keywords: food, cooking, easy, exotic, baking. Summarize. You can also have a generic boilerplate description of your channel at the bottom.

Also important are the 'end cards': these will point people to your other videos. You want them to subscribe to future content and also see past content.

It is possible to earn money from YouTube videos but you must set up an Adsense account. This enables a revenue split between you and YouTube. You can look at your ad performance report in YouTube analytics. But in the first instance, don't worry about monetization. You have to hone your skills first. You won't earn any money unless you get literally tens of thousands of views as payment is made per mille, known as RPM, or revenue per mille.

At present, there is more money in traditional media but often traditional TV, whether terrestrial, cable or satellite, gets fewer views than some YouTube channels. For this reason, traditional media is talent-scouting among YouTubers.

Building your audience

The days and hours just after you've uploaded your video are the most important in terms of building an audience and spreading the word about your channel. Again, like blogging, there is more demand during weekdays than weekends. (It seems there are an awful lot of office workers skiving off work!)

My research suggests that the optimum time to upload a YouTube video is either:

- midday on a Wednesday or Thursday, catching that peak afternoon traffic between 2 and 6 p.m. The least amount of YouTube viewing occurs between 7 p.m. and 7 a.m. (I guess when people are watching normal TV). It builds up steadily between 8 a.m. and 2 p.m.

or

- anytime at all. It doesn't matter when you upload it. It matters when you tell the world about it, 'share' it, tweet it, all that stuff. Some videos lie dormant, waiting to be discovered, then become cult. While you can do your best to hit the right time, use the right keywords, and promote it to the hilt: sometimes it's just serendipity or sheer luck that somebody discovers it and it hits a nerve.

 Key idea

That said, use your common sense. If you've done a brunch recipe, then people are more likely to search for that on a Sunday or Saturday morning. They are more likely to search for an ice cream recipe when the weather is hot and more likely to google a Christmas dinner recipe just before Christmas.

Interview with Ben Ebbrell of sorted.com

> *Sorted Food, one of the most popular YouTube channels, started four years ago. Ben set it up with three friends from university, each of whom had a different skill set: Barry Taylor (creative, branding, photography), Mike Huttlestone (production), Jamie Spafford (marketing). Ben was the only one with a food background. After self-publishing a student cookbook they decided to set up their own YouTube food channel.*

How did you get the finance to start Sorted? It's quite slick-looking.

It was much more raw in the early days. Two and a half years ago, we established a permanent studio in North London, with a full-time staff of eight people and lots of freelancers who almost work full-time. We have a whole camera team. First of all we had some money we'd earned with our cookbook. We also had sponsorship from Kenwood, who supplied product placement equipment and sponsorship.

They really took a punt on us because, four years ago, this kind of YouTube channel was innovative. We don't even have to sell their gear or mention them – their equipment is in the background, it's subliminal. We also get a small amount of advertising money from YouTube, though the ad revenue is not enough to sustain a channel.

The YouTube style has a raw feel to it. You can get away with stuff on YouTube that you couldn't on normal TV. For instance, the fridgecam. We just put a camera in the fridge and talk to it. The editing uses jump cuts. This style is very platform-centric, unique to YouTube.

I've heard that videos can really boost your stats when you blog, because YouTube is owned by Google.

YouTube is the second biggest search engine after Google, so yes. We've now made 600 videos and we have 850,000 subscribers. We make three videos a week. After a couple of years I wondered if we'd run out of ideas, but now our content is driven by the community we have on YouTube, the commenters. They come up with so many suggestions, have so many requests, we can't keep up.

How did you build up to 850,000 subscribers?

It happened in stages. First of all we invited our 50 friends on Facebook. Then we started to notice that people we didn't know were subscribing – it built to 1,000 subscribers. We also did 'collabs', collaborations, with other YouTubers. We met Charlie McDonnell who has the Charlieissocoollike channel. We asked him if we could come round to his house to cook and he said yes. So overnight our subscribers picked up from 1,000 to 5,000. We team up with other YouTubers and our audience has built up in steps. We collaborate with people who aren't in food, but that's the great thing about food, everyone is interested in it. Every collaboration we do introduces us to a new audience.

Would you recommend this to people starting a new channel on YouTube?

We were lucky – it was easier four years ago. Nowadays YouTube is much more of a machine. I'd suggest, don't jump too high. Try to do it with people who are of a similar size. Ways to meet others include going to events like Summer in the City where content creators gather. Five years ago 120 people attended. In 2014 it was held at Alexandra Palace [in North London] and 12,000 people came. We've sat on panels there. Some of the panels talk about monetization models.

So YouTube has become another TV channel really?

TV has such strict agendas – it is very hard. But now we get TV companies approaching us. However, I'd say, do it because you want to, not because you are trying to attract the attention of TV companies. Make the best content for this particular platform. We work with YouTube now, and they are using us as a case study. One of the things we are trying to persuade YouTube to do is to have a food and drink category. Every other platform has a food and drink category but we are listed under 'lifestyle' along with the fashion and beauty people. We hope that will change.

You've worked with Jamie Oliver who now has FoodTube.

We did that in 2012. This was an initiative by YouTube itself, which decided to push funds towards 'original' channels like ours. They asked Jamie to start FoodTube and helped fund it. We collaborated with him, which helped to attract viewers towards his new channel and also helped us with our profile.

Key idea

You can't control the Zeitgeist. As Ben Ebbrell of Sorted says, 'You don't set out to make a viral video, you just make videos and one of them may catch on and go viral. The nearest we ever got to it was using themes; people love a theme like *Game of Thrones*. Another time we got near to it was when we did cronuts.'

Next step

In the final chapter we will look at the future of food writing. Is it bleak or is there cause for optimism?

12

The future of food writing

The future of food writing may seem bleak. Newspapers and magazines are losing money, often closing down, and nobody knows how long print media is going to last. Look at your own reading habits: do you still buy newspapers and magazines or do you read their content online? (This applies particularly to newspapers, as magazines, rather like cookbooks, are often bought for their aesthetic appeal.) With the demise of print media, will there still be a role for food writers?

Yes, of course. But the whole sector will move online. Ironically, it's bloggers who are responsible for this to a certain extent. Blogging started off as a stepping stone to a food writing career but is also one of the factors in why a paid food writing career is increasingly difficult to achieve.

There are also questions about how to monetize online writing – either by charging for advertising, or sponsored content, or by running food events. The money remains a problem for those who don't have a private income and do not want to keep their food writing as a hobby. This issue was tackled in Chapter 9.

Regarding the publishing industry, the future of cookbooks looks remarkably buoyant, although people tend to buy cookbooks as gifts rather than as a method of instruction like a manual. According to literary agent Michael Alcock of Johnson & Alcock, many books are financed via co-editions – that is, they are sold to other countries prior to being published; this way the publisher knows that the book will sell a certain amount. The emphasis on co-editions means that there must be no text in photos, as it can't be translated without reshooting and food writing has to be international and less localized in style and vocabulary. In the United States, where they have such a large market domestically, this is not so much the case.

A cookbook is very expensive to produce, around £50,000. It has to earn that back in the first two years if possible. (Books that don't work are a tax write-off for publishers, however.)

Who buys books? There are two main markets: trophy buyers and foodies, says Alcock. What he means by 'trophy' buyers is those who want a beautiful object, a coffee-table book. And the other audience is foodies, especially women. Young people buy in pre-prepared food; they don't really cook until they set up home permanently. They will spend their spare income on going out, hair, clothes and make-up. The exception is baking: many young people will buy a baking cookbook, a kind of leisure cookery that they can do on the weekends.

'The beautiful cookbook will endure,' says Alcock. As a result, food photographers and book designers are more important nowadays than they used to be. Cookbooks are visually driven.

New ways of teaching and talking about food

Food content producers – that is, those of us who want to write, talk about and create food – are increasingly looking for alternative media through which to make a living and diversify our outlets. For learning how to cook, people are turning to online resources such as step-by-step blog posts and detailed 'How tos' with advice from one amateur cook to another.

The food channel Sorted (see Chapter 12) on YouTube is an inspirational way to produce a cooking show without depending on the mainstream media. It has innovated a new method and platform for food content. Jamie's FoodTube now gets 9 million views and has a roster of home-grown stars. Established chefs such as Valentine Warner, who previously had mainstream terrestrial TV series (on the BBC), is now presenting videos for Jamie's FoodTube.

Apps are yet to come of age, although top food writers/cooks such as Jamie Oliver, Nigella Lawson and Mario Batali have invested in pretty sophisticated apps. Apps and ebooks, if they use video, can be expensive to produce, at present sequential static photographs are useful and more economical.

Many food writers are now issuing their own ebooks and this sector will only expand as more people buy tablets. It's estimated that the market for tablets will outstrip that of desktop computers and laptops soon. The iPad is particularly useful in the kitchen: you can have the video playing while you are cooking and you don't need to worry about splashing the keyboard or screen.

Key idea

Increasingly food writers and cooks are creating apps. The monetization model relies more on volume than high unit prices. However, this is an area the budding food writer should not ignore. The hugely popular Deliciously Ella (Eleanor Woodward), a young food blogger whose healthy diet has improved her health, made an app that went to number one in the app charts.

Tim Hayward, author of *DIY Food* and food editor at the *Financial Times*, doesn't think one needs expensively produced TV programmes and videos. A grainy video on YouTube, filmed with a smartphone, is just as compelling as Jamie Oliver, he thinks.

He continues: 'Trip Advisor reviews have made restaurant reviewing redundant and the Internet has made recipe writing for print media pointless.' Tim believes that there are no new recipes. He notes the change in cookbooks away from food writing and the personality of the food writer to just pure recipes with no context and no introduction. Again, this makes selling co-editions abroad easier. I personally have experienced this: in my cookbook *V is for Vegan*, I've had to fight to keep in the introductory chapter talking about why people may consider a vegan diet. The publisher would have preferred just recipes and pictures.

Tim comments further: 'The way that cookbooks are laid out, you can flick through them quickly, perhaps put a sticky note on recipes that catch your eye, put it back on the shelf and feel as if you've consumed that book. You may never break the spine of that book.' He also points out that, even if you get a book deal, you are only likely to get a decent, liveable advance if you have a TV programme attached. 'Today 85 per cent of a book advance is attached to whether you get a TV programme. With my book *DIY Food*, I sold 9,000 copies, a respectable amount, but if I'd got TV, that would have been 90,000.' This means that most TV production companies are reluctant to pay for onscreen talent. I've been offered opportunities to be on TV that I've turned down because they wouldn't pay.

Catherine Phipps, author of *The Pressure Cooker Cookbook*, however, is optimistic about the future of food writing, although she acknowledges that, in order to earn a living, one needs other ways of adding to one's income such as a shop (Sally Butcher, author of *Veggiestan* and *Snackistan*), hiring out one's kitchen for photo-shoots and writing a column (Diana Henry, author of *Crazy Water, Pickled Lemons*), copyediting (Hattie Ellis, author of *A Spoonful of Honey*), supper clubs (myself) or ghostwriting (not allowed to say).

Catherine often reviews cookbooks and says, 'Every year cookbooks come out that genuinely excite me.' There is still so much to write about, new techniques, new cuisines. For instance, there isn't much food writing about African cuisine, which has a very different repertoire of ingredients, unless it's North African food. There are intriguing hybrid and fusion cookbooks to be explored, and books such as *Bitter* by Jennifer MacLagen, which looks at the much neglected bitter end of the food spectrum.

Of course, it's a challenge to create entirely new recipes, and some books are merely rehashing old recipes, but, with new ingredients from world cuisine and innovative scientifically influenced techniques, cooking is constantly evolving. The microwave became a common household bit of kit from the 1980s onwards, and this has changed how people cook (possibly for the worse, though it remains useful for quick defrosting, tempering chocolate and so on). Who knows what the next couple of decades will bring in terms of 21st-century technology for both dining and cooking?

I asked Stefan Chomka, editor of *Restaurant Magazine*, what he considers to be the future of food writing, mentioning Marina O'Loughlin's comment that to get a job as a restaurant critic, it's a case of dead men's shoes. 'The big salaries that are paid to the important food writers, that's not sustainable. When they go (as in leave or die) the position will go, or the publication goes. The papers will get an intern who will do it for peanuts or axe it, just like the *Metro*.' The *Metro* newspaper sacked their entire food reviewing staff. Both Stefan and I agreed that we thought this was a mistake for a London paper. 'Yes, it's not like the *Metro* restaurant reviewers were paid much. They go once to review, not six times, like they do in the USA where they take it all much more seriously.'

American restaurant critics consider themselves to have a 'duty of care'. Here, in the UK, most food writing is entertainment. For instance, Michael Winner's restaurant column in the *Sunday Times* wasn't about the food; it was about whom he was with. It was supercilious but entertaining. It was showbiz.

Stefan is rather pessimistic about the future of good-quality food writers: 'Yes. Now owners are all about output and headlines. They'd rather get a columnist who has a name. Look at Pippa Middleton who is now a food columnist for *Waitrose Kitchen*. If you've got that celebrity angle as well, it's another string to your bow. The celebrity food writer is a logical progression from the celebrity chef culture.

Is there any cause for optimism? 'People are always going to eat out. There will always be something to write about,' says Stefan.' However, that doesn't mean that you can make a living from food writing. 'Things are changing all the time. Look at Buzzfeed and Vice; it's all online journalism. They must be making money.' Buzzfeed now seem to have political journalists reporting from places like Ukraine so it's expanding its remit from gifs, 'ten best of lists' and jokey summations of pop culture. (Buzzfeed has been very influenced by Tumblr.) Munchies, the food channel of vice.com, is investing in food writing and food videos.

But so often the presenters of food TV and videos will not be food experts but young, pretty people who have good presenting skills. Or producers will want a panel of experts, based on the *Top Gear* model. Tim Hayward is about to appear on *Daily Brunch*, a new Channel 4 TV programme: 'They don't have any cooking facilities; they say they can't get it passed by health and safety.' So everything is either faked 'or you just talk about how to do it which is strange for a programme about brunch'.

Another area of interest is specialist food magazines such as *Lucky Peach*, *Gastronomica*, the annual food edition of the *New Yorker* and, launched in the UK in 2014, an annual food writing magazine called *Toast* featuring writing, photography and illustration.

 ## Sally Whittle from Foodies100

'The platform may change in the future, people may be perhaps microblogging on Instagram. But it doesn't matter what the platform is as long as you've got a website. Online food writing is here to stay.'

The future also lies in interacting with PRs and marketing departments. Remember, PRs will not pay you but will give you stuff for free. You want to be in their good books but not compromise your content around their agenda. In the seven years I've been blogging, I've seen the rise of the influence of PRs on blogging and, in fact, all journalism. An organization called PR Watch logs this influence on the mainstream media; in some cases, journalists just copy press releases and issue them as news. A good PR such as Dominique Fraser of Fraser Communications will pitch stories about their clients, with interesting angles, to the right publication. She's presenting the story on a plate for the journalists and this is increasingly necessary in view of shrinking staff levels in the media.

Good PRs are appreciated by journalists and bloggers. Bad PRs will have a scattergun approach, spamming their entire mailing list with inappropriate material. I can't tell you the amount of times I've been offered stories or product from meat companies when it says on my blog that I don't cook or eat meat. (This is also a good reason to have a very clear statement in your 'About me' tab about what you do and don't cover, even if you don't have a full media pack.) Increasingly, the food writer and even the food blogger is working with PRs, it's the lay of the land.

Money, money, money

Food writing has always been the preserve of the leisured classes, those who have a trust fund to rely on and who don't need the money to survive. Tim Hayward comments: 'You don't have to be posh to be a food writer but you do to be able to continue for longer than two weeks!'

Recipe creation and food PR are two fields in which you will be paid. I've just earned more for writing six recipes for a company than I have for writing this book. A position in food PR means that you will get a salary you can depend on. Being a freelancer is tough, isolating and insecure and most food writing is freelance.

Working for trade publications is another route into salaried work connected with the food industry. Readers who need to earn a living at what they do should consider these options.

Neil Davey, freelance travel and food journalist

'At some point, someone is going to make online pay. Newspapers are going behind pay walls or go free and rely on advertising.'

Other future areas of expansion in terms of food writing

One might imagine that with a growing world population, under pressure from agribusiness and GMOs, food writing will be increasingly about diversity and health. The impact on our health system from obesity, which can lead to diseases such as diabetes 2, means that we have to think more seriously about health and nutrition and the wider implications of food writing. So there is the food writing that is about nice meals (which is important) but also the really essential educational stuff, which is a whole lot less glamorous. This is food writing that is about how to eat so that we don't die early and in pain; how to eat so that we don't end up on dialysis; how to eat so that we don't get cancer; how to eat so that we don't end up on a drugs regimen of several medicines a day for the rest of our lives. Anyone writing and researching about this kind of food is not going to be out of work anytime soon.

Opinions about food are something we all have, and writing down those opinions is always going to be a feature, whether it be recipe writing, food politics, health writing or restaurant reviews. With the ubiquitous Instagramming of what we eat, food blogging, the sharing of dinners on Facebook, one could say food writing has almost become commonplace. The problem is, everybody is an expert and there are few specialists. Food writing comes under lifestyle as a subject and the kind of geeky informed food writer that food obsessives might aspire to be doesn't have a commercial market.

Nonetheless, the downside of food is also the upside: food will always be a necessary, integral part of human existence. What we consume, we document, one way or another: food writing will always have an audience.

Index

Acton, Eliza, 46
advances, 144, 147–8
agents, 147, 150–1
Alcock, Michael, 149–51, 190
Amazon, 158–9
anecdotes, 60
Apple, 158–9
apps, 191
archives, 77–8
Armendariz, Matt, 116
Authors' Licensing and Collecting Society (ALCS), 148
awards, 145–6

Badger, Emily, 23
Baldwin, Jan, 128
Barham, Dr Peter, 38
Beckett, Fiona, 40
Beeton, Mrs, 46
Bertinet, Richard, 29
Best-Shaw, Helen, 88–90, 94
Blogger, 68
blogging, 66–94 (see also social media)
  book reviews, 144
  earning money, 135–42
  blog rolls, 75
Blumenthal, Heston, 163
book deals, 147, 150–7
book reviews, 144
Bourdain, Anthony, 49
branding, 96–7
Brillat-Savarin, Jean, Anthelme, 46

British Indian Restaurant (BIR) food, 10
Buford, Bill, 49
Buzzfeed, 193–4

Carême, Marie-Antoine, 46
Cazals, Jean, 128
characteristics of food writers, 8–15
Child, Julia, 48
Chomka, Stefan, 41, 193
Cleese, John, 100
Clerkenwellboy, 107
clichés to avoid, 22
Cloake, Felicity, 115
comments on your blog, 71–2
conferences, 109
cookbooks, 154–5
  copyright, 34–5
  future, 190–3
  history, 44
  introductions, 25–6
  writing, 24–34, 161–2
cookies disclaimers, 73
cooking, 9–10
  courses, 13–14
  methods, 30–1
copyright, 34–5, 73–4, 76
Coren, Giles, 19, 99–100
cover design, 156–7
Craddock, Fanny, 47
crowdfunding, 160–1
curries, 9–10

Davey, Neil, 139–42, 195
David, Elizabeth, 47, 116
Davies, Katie Quinn, 116
Day, Ivan, 41
De Bernières, Louis, 145
design, 156–7
  of blogs, 78–81
diet writing, 39
Dillon, Sheila, 166–9
domain names, 68
drinks, 39–40

Ebbrell, Ben, 185–7
ebooks, 157–61, 191
editors, 155
Eleven Madison Park, 18
Ephron, Nora, 48
equipment list, 26–7
Escoffier, Georges Auguste, 46

Facebook, 97, 103–4
Faulkner, William, 54
Fearnley-Whittingstall, Hugh, 48
fees for writing, 132–3, 135–42, 195
fermentation, 38
festivals, 144–5
Fisher, Mary, 48
Foer, Jonathan Safran, 36
food essays, 36

The Food Programme
(BBC Radio 4),
166–7
Fortnum & Mason, 146
freebies, 72, 83

Gaye, Dr Morgaine, 36
Ghaynour, Sabrina, 45
ghostwriting, 162–3
Gill, A.A., 19
Glasse, Hannah, 46, 116
Google Ads, 135
Google Plus, 108
Google tools, 69
Goyoaga, Aran, 116
Graves, Helen, 87–8
Greeks, ancient, 45
Grey, Patience and
    Primrose Boyd, 47
Grigson, Jane, 47
Guild of Food Writers,
    146

hashtags, 101, 106
Hay, Donna, 114
Hayward, Tim, 147–8,
    191–2, 194, 195
health books, 39
Heath, Ambrose, 47
Hemingway, Ernest,
    12–13
history of food, 41
history of food writing,
    44–9
Hom, Ken, 45
honesty, 12

identity online, 96–7
ingredients list, 27
Instagram, 106–8
international cuisine, 15,
    44–5
Internet videos, 185–6

making, 170–81
    uploading, 181–4
interviews, 58–9

Jacob, Diane, 55
Jaffrey, Madhur, 45
Johansen, Signe, 45
Jones, Liz, 12
Jonsson, Mikael, 137

Kamozawa, Aki & H.
    Alexander Talbot,
    38
Katz, Sandor Ellix, 38–9
Keogan, Eva, 102–3
Kholi, Hardeep Singh,
    101
Kimbell, Vanessa, 166
King, Stephen, 24

language
    clichés to avoid, 22
    cooking methods,
        30–1
    readability, 26
Lawrence, Felicity, 36
Lawson, Nigella, 25–6,
    28, 47, 163
Lebowitz, David, 28, 33,
    35, 71, 151
Leith, Prue, 47
Lepard, Dan, 115
Lewin, Regula, 116
libel, 24, 76–7
licensing laws, 73–4
links, online, 74–6
Llewin, Regula, 41
Lloyd, Vivien and Nigel,
    158–60
Loftus, David, 128
Lowe, Jason, 128

magazines, 194

Márquez, Gabriel
    García, 60
Martin, James, 27
Maschler, Fay, 19
Matalon-Degni,
    Francine, 115
McGee, Harold, 48
McGinn, Helen, 40
measurements, 27–30
Mickler, Ernest Mathew,
    56
Middle Ages food
    writing, 45–6
Monroe, Jack, 11
Moran, Caitlin, 55
Myhrvold, Nathan, 39,
    115

networking, 144–5
newsletters, 82
newspapers, reviews,
    18–21
Nilssen, Magnus, 44

O'Loughlin, Marina,
    19, 98
Observer Food Monthly,
    146
Oikawa, Keiko, 128
Oliver, Jamie, 154, 175,
    186, 191
Orwell, George, 62
Ottolenghi, Yotam and
    Sami Tamimi, 48,
    149
ovens, 32–3

Peltre, Béatrice, 116
Phipps, Catherine,
    161–2, 192
photography, 114–17,
    128–9
    editing, 126–7

equipment, 117–18
presentation, 123–6
techniques, 118–22
Pinterest, 104–5
pitching, 133–5
politics, 11
Pollan, Michael, 36, 49
Pople, Chris, 90–4
Powell, Julia, 48
PR companies, 83–4, 194–5
proposals, 151–2
Public Lending Right (PLR), 148
publishing industry, 190
publishing process, 153–5
publishing team, 155–6

Qin Xie, 37, 40

radio programmes, 166–9
Rayner, Jay, 19, 24
recipe writing, 24–5, 154–5
copyright, 34–5
history, 44
instructions, 26–34
introductions, 25–6
Renton, Alex, 11
restaurant reviews, 18–24, 72, 193
restaurants, opening, 137
Reynière, Grimod de la, 46
Robinson, Gary, 101–2
Roden, Claudia, 47, 154
Rodgers, Kerstin, 115–16
Romans, 45
Romero, Terry Hope, 28

routine, 53–4, 161
royalties, 144
Ruhlman, Michael, 29, 49
Rundell, Mrs, 46

Salter, Katy, 39, 133–5
Sbuttoni, Anna, 40
scientific approach to food preparation, 38–9
Segnit, Niki, 149
self-publishing, 157–61
Sexton, David, 25
Sheasby, Anne, 154–5
Shields, Niamh, 98, 160
Slater, Nigel, 25–6, 33, 47, 163
sleeper hits, 149
Smith, Delia, 31, 47
social media, 67–8, 72, 83–4, 96–109 see also blogging
specialist food writing, 40–1
sponsored posts, 136, 138–9
Stekelman, Greg, 98
style of writing, 54–63
Sugura, Yuki, 128
Supper Club (Rodgers), 34–5, 153

tags, 74
technical food preparation, 38–9
temperatures, 32–3
Tilson, Jake, 158
titles of books, 160
Toombs, Dan, 9–10, 108, 110–11
trade press, 40–1

training, 13–15
travel writing, 37
trends, 36
Trip Advisor, 21
trolling, 72
Tumblr, 69
TV shows, 150, 169–70 see also videos
Twitter, 97–103

umami (savouriness), 38
Unbound, 161
United States
history of food writing, 48–9
measurements, 28
utensils, sizes, 31

videos, 185–6
making, 170–81
uploading, 181–4
Vimeo, 171
vocabulary see language
voice, 25, 57, 59–61

Walker, Esther, 10
Waters, Alice, 28, 48
White, Florence, 47
Whittle, Sally, 83, 85–6, 194
Wilson, Bee, 57
Winch-Furness, Paul, 128
wine, 39–40
WordPress, 68
Workman, Caroline, 24

Young British Foodies, 146
YouTube, 139, 170–1, 173, 181–6 see also videos

Acknowledgements

The author and publisher would like to thank the following people for their valuable contributions to this book: Michael Alcock of johnsonandalcock.co.uk; Helen Best-Shaw of fussfreeflavours.com; Stefan Chomka of Restaurant magazine;

Neil Davey of The Bluffer's Guide to Chocolate and The Bluffer's Guide to Food; Sheila Dillon of BBC Radio 4's The Food Programme; Ben Ebbrell of sorted.com; Helen Graves of foodstories.com; Tim Hayward; Jeanne Horak-Druiff of cooksister.com; Eva Keogan of homeofsocial.com; Vivien and Nigel Lloyd of vivienlloyd.com; Krista Madden of handpicked. com; Marina O'Loughlin; Catherine Phipps; Chris Pople of cheeseandbiscuits.com; Qin Xie; Katy Salter; Dan Toombs, The Curry Guy of greatcurryrecipes.net; and Sally Whittle of foodies100.com.